KISSING KEVIN

AN AMERICAN NURSE IN THE VIETNAM WAR

BY SARA BERG

CIRQUE PRESS

Cirque Press
Copyright ©2024 Edward Berg

All rights reserved. No part of this publication may be reproduced, distributed or transmitted in any form or by any means, including photocopying, recording, or other electronic or mechanical methods, without the prior written permission of the publisher and author, except in the case of brief quotations embodied in critical reviews and certain other noncommercial uses permitted by copyright law.

Published by
Cirque Press

Sandra Kleven — Michael Burwell
3157 Bettles Bay Loop
Anchorage, AK 99515

Print ISBN:
979-889480364-7

cirquejournal@gmail.com
www.cirquejournal.com

Cover art by Kevin G. Smith Photography and Moontide Design
Back cover author photo by Edward Berg
Layout by Moontide Design

DEDICATION

This book is dedicated to my mother who loved me unconditionally and taught me to be compassionate by her example. Also to my daughter Duffy, a compassionate woman, dearly loved and taken from us way too soon by the hand of evil. You both inspired me to write this book. You are both now at peace, but you left so much love behind. You are in every breath I take.

TABLE OF CONTENTS

Dedication

Foreword

Chapter 1
  Kissing Kevin — 3
  Arrival in Country — 9

Chapter 2
  The Vegetable Garden — 15
  Positive Joe — 28
  The Boy with No Face — 29
  Louie the Heartbreaker — 29

Chapter 3
  The Babies — 35
  A Baby Story in Pictures — 55

Chapter 4
  Wards 2 and 3 — 63

Chapter 5
  The Burn Unit — 71

Chapter 6 — This and That
  Rest and Recuperation — 81
  Larry the Lobster — 82
  Shit Happens — 84
  The Atrocious Bob Hope Show — 85
  Underwear — 87
  The Tank — 90

Chapter 7 — Where Was the Compassion?

    Careless Homicide   95

    A Powerful Patriarch   96

    Stand Up to the Haughty   98

    Child Soldier   99

    Kidnapped Baby   99

Chapter 8 — Patti's Story

    A Slow Day at The War   105

    Second Tour and After   107

    Upon This Wall   110

Epilogue

Appendix

FOREWORD

The reader of this story will wonder why I ever went to Vietnam. Youth, ignorance, and gullibility all played big parts.

I was an officer's army brat, one of six kids. I loved living on Army bases and had no negative connotations about the armed forces. I went to private catholic schools and all-girl high schools and nursing school, and was pretty sheltered. I feel that I have never fully recovered from the horrors of those schools and nuns, and that I was well indoctrinated by them.

The Army nurse corps recruiters were relentless; they came to the nursing schools and focused on the senior class. They made it sound so patriotic and glorious. We would be heroines. It made me recall the countless movies about World War II. The nurse saving lives, the handsome soldier whisking her off her feet, all living happily ever after. All so untrue.

The other motivator was money. I had none; my parents barely scraped together my school tuition. The Army would pay the last year's tuition, and I would get the phenomenal sum of $300/month for just going to school.

Another factor was that I wanted to go to midwifery school, which required two years nursing experience, and this was a two-year hitch with the Army. Many of my nursing school classmates joined, so why shouldn't I? We had no idea how this decision would change our lives forever!

I want to thank my precious husband Ed Berg for enabling me to write this book. He is my rock, and, as our daughter once said, "a convenience store of tranquility." He has been right by my side holding me up for these past many years of slogging through our nightmare of losing our daughter. On October 17, our 38-year-old daughter disappeared from the streets of our hometown of Homer, Alaska. She was walking to a medical appointment. For two and a half years we knew nothing about her disappearance, only our searches, our pleas, our aloneness, the agony of so many questions. Ed let me be me, in my agony, never directing, only supporting. Last year, after the truth was revealed and the horror of how she was murdered and disposed of came out, he held me up and kept me afloat. I wanted to follow her; he wanted me by his side, to find purpose in life again. And so I have, by writing this book that has been trying to burst out of me for fifty years. It just wrote itself. If this was not your Vietnam, so be it; it was mine and writing it has brought me great comfort.

DISTANCES FROM THE 24TH EVAC HOSPITAL AT LONG BINH:

- Saigon center – *30 miles southwest*
- Tan Son Nhat airbase – *28 miles southwest*
- Bien Hoa – *5 miles northwest*
- Vung Tau – *66 miles south*
- Cam Ranh Bay – *270 miles northeast*

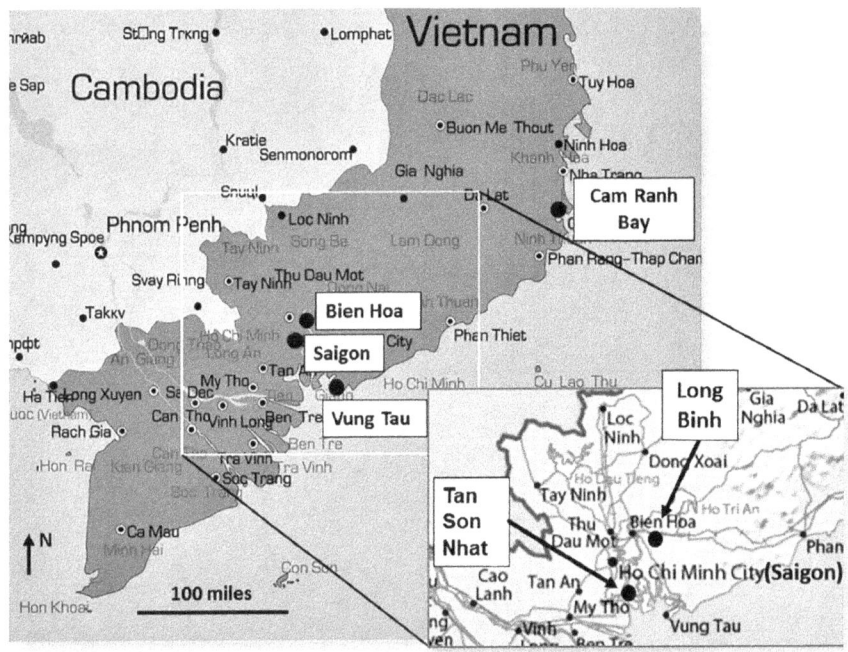

Map credits: OrangeSmile.com and GISGeography.com

24TH EVAC HOSPITAL, LONG BINH, VIETNAM, C.1971

Photo credit: http://www.24thevacuationhospital.org/History/1971_history.htm

CHAPTER 1

KISSING KEVIN

Yes, it's true. I gave Kevin the longest juiciest most heartfelt kiss I had ever given anyone. It was June 1st, 1971, early in the morning. It was a strange kiss in many ways; he was lying flat on his back naked. A slim sheet for modesty's sake covered part of him, as we were in a very public place. I was fully dressed, standing up leaning over him, my right hand imbedded in his light brown curls. He asked for that kiss, and I gave it quite willingly. It was the last thing he ever did, and asking for it were his last words. It was the most memorable kiss I have ever had. He was 21 and I was 22. I had only known him for three days.

I remember well our first meeting, but I was introduced earlier by phone. My nurse friend Patti Hill called the day before and asked how busy our ward was. I was in the Intensive Care burn unit; she was in the recovery room. She had a patient for me but was reluctant to give him up; she had grown quite fond of him and wanted to be sure that he got the best of care. I told her that we had very few patients and could handle him fine. Even so, she was a bit greedy and didn't send him over until the end of her shift. Why miss a minute with him? Often it was like that, we got so attached so easily.

I was there when Kevin arrived, just finishing up my paperwork from my 12-hour shift. The new crew on my ward greeted him, and the old crew from the recovery room delivered him on their way back to their beds. There were probably six people in the two crews. All extremely busy getting him settled. He was put right next to the nurses' desk, as he was the sickest. I looked up from my papers to see why there were so many people and so much activity. The first thing I saw was Kevin's terror-filled face. I ran to the head of his bed and put my hands on the sides of his face and bent down and whispered in his ear, "Kevin, it's OK. I'm Sara and I won't leave you. You're in good hands. They are all experts. They know what they are doing." I stayed an extra hour and talked him through every maneuver, sitting on the floor so he could see my face. He was on a Stryker frame and was being turned over for the first time — a terrifying event for him and all of us.

A Stryker frame is a very skinny bed for paralyzed people so they can be turned over. With them lying on their backs, another skinny bed is placed on top of them and bolted down, and then three straps are cinched around the two beds with the patient in the middle like a sandwich. Two people — one at the head and the other at the foot — flip them over and remove the top bed. Usually, the beds are turned every two hours to help with circulation and prevent bedsores. Most patients hate being face down, as they can see nothing but the floor and it's isolating and often more painful.

OK, so why was this so difficult with Kevin? Every few hours we flipped several Strykers; we could do it in our sleep. Well, Kevin was special. He had more tubes and machines attached to him than any of us had ever seen. Every tube needed to remain attached and functioning to keep him alive. We had to be sure of where every tube would land after the flip; there was no room for error. We had to go slowly and carefully and, quite frankly, the crew was scared. When it was completed, the team was shaking and hugging one another. I meanwhile never stopped whispering in his ear, to keep him calm and unable to hear the nervous crew.

A trach tube kept him from speaking to me, but his eyes said it all; our communication was great. The tubes, as I remember them, were a respirator hooked to a trach tube, a naso-gastric tube, two chest tubes, three IV's — one a central line, a Foley catheter, and two wound drainage bags. There was no cardiac monitor, as we had none on the wards, and no oxygen saturation monitors, as they had not been invented yet. We had a giant oxygen tank and a suction machine beside the bed.

Once Kevin was settled on his tummy, with all the tubes working well, I wished him and my co-workers well and walked in the broiling heat to my nice, air-conditioned hooch for a good day's sleep. Not really expecting to see Kevin again. Eleven hours later at 7 p.m. I was back.

Not only was Kevin alive, he remembered me! We also heard from headquarters that his father, a high-ranking officer, was in country and heading our way. We were all over the moon with joy! My fondest wish daily, while caring for these dying boys was that I was their loving mother, not me, some strange nurse.

At this time the war was slowly winding down, so we had only four patients in the ICU, with two nurses and two corpsmen. This was an unheard-of situation, as usually we had 17 patients. I was assigned to Kevin solo; what a treat! He required a LOT of care, but I could take lots of time and give him all those extra touches to make him feel special. He couldn't feel anything from the neck down and couldn't talk unless I covered his trach tube, but he felt the cheek caresses and head rubs. He could see the winks and hear the stories. He could answer with eye blinks; I could explain everything to him. I could give him what I wanted to give them all, but never had the time. I used to run down a full ward trying to touch as many toes as possible, letting those boys know I was thinking of them even though I couldn't stop, because someone else needed me more.

That first night I cared for Kevin he indicated that he had something to say. I covered the tracheotomy tube; "Captain Patti" is all he said, meaning my recovery room friend Patti that I had been thinking of all day. I kept the tears back because I knew that Patti had just been admitted to the hospital for a suicide attempt. It was her second tour in Vietnam, and it was rough for her. I stopped by her ward the next morning on the way home to bed. I told her that dying was not an option; she had an important job to do. Kevin needed her; he might have only a few hours left. She jumped right out of bed and the doldrums she was in and ran across the hospital to be with him. She spent several hours with him, caressing his hair, smiling and telling stories, pulling herself and him right up. To this day she is my dear friend, the most compassionate person I know.

The next night Kevin was slipping in and out of consciousness, and I once again got him to myself. The day nurses said they had heard no word from the father, and they were pretty sure Kevin wouldn't get through the night. I gave him the best of care with him mostly unconscious and me sitting holding his soft hair whenever I had a break. Early that morning he awoke and asked for that kiss, and then slipped back into his coma. He died that morning after I had gone to bed, another nurse by his side.

Well, unbeknownst to me, that kiss caused an uproar. I hadn't seen the chief nurse making her rounds while I was kissing Kevin. At report, an hour later, I was told to report to the chief nurse immediately. I was in trouble. Certainly not the first time; I was a rule breaker and fond of doing things my way, especially when it seemed to make way more sense.

I was torn apart for a half an hour; not only had I kissed Kevin on an open ward for all to see (especially those four other sleeping patients) but I had the audacity to kiss an *enlisted* man. I was an officer; how dare I do that and in public no less? I went back to my ward right after my brow beating, not the least repentant. I told the crew what had transpired with the chief. I kissed sweet Kevin on his forehead and went to bed. That night at 7, I was back on shift. Sadly, Kevin was gone, and I never heard anything of his father. There was however a new category posted on the care board: "Hugs and kisses PRN." PRN means "when necessary." All the patients had a check mark in that new category. To make things more official, the Doc's even wrote orders in every chart. The nurses were happy to oblige, and the patients received that extra attention eagerly.

In June of 1985 I was living in Alaska and saw that the traveling Vietnam Memorial Wall was coming to Kenai, just two hours away. I spent several hours at the wall, running my fingers over all the names I knew, including Kevin's. The book that came with the wall said he was from a small town in Washington where his parents lived. I found their number and called them. I talked to both parents and a sister; they wanted the story told over and over again. I sent them pictures of Kevin as well; I don't imagine that they were easy to see.

We heard a lot about dying alone during COVID, but never during the war. These boys were 18 years old, and I sat with as many as I could while they died. Mostly I knew nothing about them, but I always thought of their families and talked about their families as they left. I could never substitute for their mothers, but I did my best.

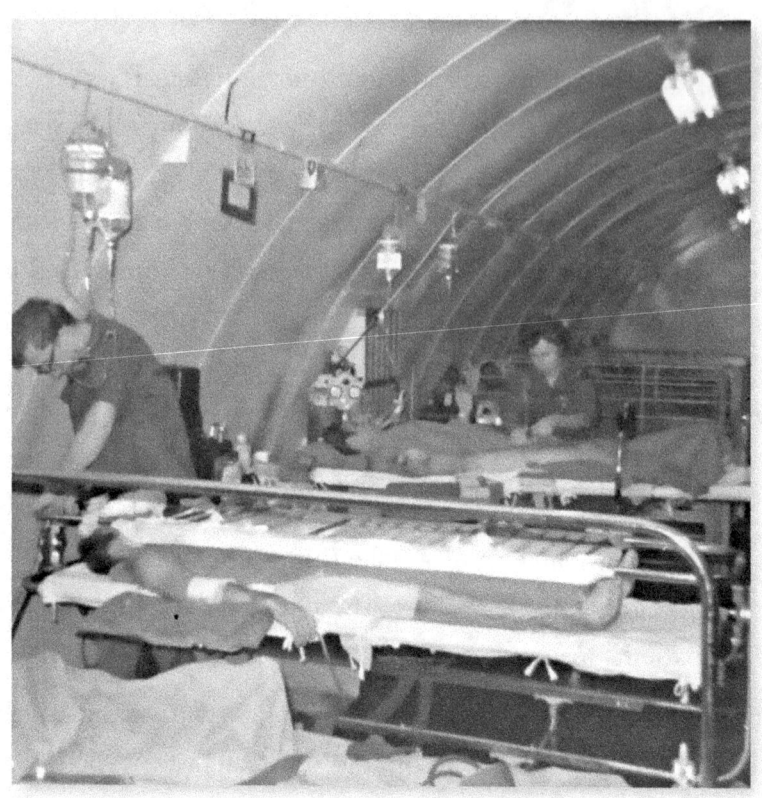

A Stryker frame being bolted down. It will then be cinched with three straps and flipped by two people. The top bed is then removed. This was done every two hours, although most patients begged to be left facing up. We felt bad ignoring their pleas; they had never seen a bedsore but we had, so a bit of tough love was necessary.

ARRIVAL IN COUNTRY

I was late. I missed my plane to Vietnam! I was certainly not taking all the Army rules seriously. They told us at basic training that we were officers first, nurses second and women third. I certainly never believed that order, which is probably why I didn't stay in the service and probably why I was never asked to. The army really needed nurses, so they overlooked that defiant little part of me.

Well, I was only a little bit late. Maybe they wouldn't notice after all. The airport was mobbed, men and boys everywhere, not an empty seat or a woman to be seen. I had been on an adventure to Lassen State Park in northern California with a friend and we either lost track of time or it was the traffic; I can't remember. I do remember discussing with my friend about the consequences of being late, and we decided the worst they could do was send me to Vietnam, so I figured I was all set. They weren't going to discharge me, not after all that recruiting. In fact, I don't remember that they even noticed. Just told me my flight left in the morning. So there I was dressed in my summer officers uniform, complete with skirt, stockings and heels. I remember putting them on in the car on the way to the airport.

My bag was checked, so I just had a purse, and tons and tons of time on my hands. I was in a gigantic room filled to the brim with young, excited and perhaps a bit anxious men. I of course had a book with me, so I found a corner and read for hours, keeping the men at bay, avoiding eye contact. By evening I was exhausted and needed desperately to sleep. I swept my eyes around the room, looking for a location and a protective partner. I approached a young innocent looking soldier and sounded him out. I found that he was on my flight, and I felt I could trust him, so I asked him to be my sleeping partner. In other words, I wanted to sleep next to a wall with him next to me, protecting me from advances. We spent the night side by side, sleeping as peacefully as possible in that madhouse.

The next morning, we were on our 20-hour flight to Vietnam. Every seat of course was full and I had a middle one. The first thing I did was shed the heels, and all I remember of the flight was the harried hostess who was nice to me. We arrived at Tan Son Nhat airbase right after dark and the plane became very quiet as reality set in.

Someone from the airbase boarded the plane and announced that they had taken enemy fire within the last 24 hours, and we needed to get in the hanger as fast as we could, zig-zagging as we ran. How was that possible? I was exhausted after a 20-hour flight that followed a hard night at the airport that followed a two-day camping trip! To top it off I had heels; they were low but useless because I absolutely could not get them onto my super swollen feet. I would need to run in nylon stockings but made it in quickly for a nice long wait for transport by convoy to Bien Hoa reception center. Before leaving, we were given instructions on what to do if the convoy was attacked. This was getting dicier by the minute, and I just wanted to get somewhere safe and sleep.

We had a right to be a bit anxious. I learned later that six months earlier, a soldier on the way home after his injury-free year of service was sitting at the airport when it was bombed, leaving him with no legs and just one arm.

Sleep came well after midnight after we had all our money

exchanged for fake bills and had heard endless speeches that I don't remember. We were issued our clothing and boots in duffle bags and given our assignments. I really kept thinking that they should have let us sleep and then we would have absorbed some of this important information much better. However, it was another sleepless night spent in a women's dormitory where an excited group of nurses was getting ready to fly out at 3 a.m. for their assignments up north. The next morning, I was taking the tour of the 24th Evac Hospital and assigned to the Vegetable Garden, without a soul mentioning I was a day late.

Welcome to Vietnam!

CHAPTER 2

THE VEGETABLE GARDEN

After a one-day debriefing in Bien Hoa I was assigned to the 24th Evacuation Hospital in Long Binh, which was one of two hospitals on a ten-mile square of defoliated earth surrounded by barbed wire.

Quonset huts were used to build the hospital, arranged in a rectangle. Bathrooms and hallways connected all the huts, and a covered outdoor walkway went around the inside of the rectangle. A bare-earth courtyard was in the middle. The Agent Orange defoliant did an excellent job of keeping us from having any interactions with plant life.

I was assigned to the neurosurgical Wards 5 and 6 right after my initial tour of the hospital on Day One. These wards took care of head and spinal cord injuries. During the tour, I had decided that those wards would be my last choice. I had to keep a stiff upper lip when the chief told me my fate. I could do it. I could learn. Little did I know that the learning would be easy, compared to the repair of the broken heart.

Early in my tour of duty, the big chief at the hospital decided that the hospital grounds needed sprucing up. The plan was that the staff would plant flowers in front of the wards facing the inner courtyard. I think seeds had been sent by some well-meaning relative. You can't grow anything in Agent Orange soil, so this was an exercise in futility. Agent Orange has caused thousands of birth defects and cancers in soldiers of both sides, civilians, and their offspring. It is still happening today in Vietnam. The soil is still contaminated, but people have to grow crops in order to eat. Another U.S. disgrace.

We nurses, however, were given orders to try, so we got down in that contaminated dirt and put in those seeds. Our ward decided to plant vegetables, as most of the patients on the neurosurgical intensive care unit were in a vegetative state and we used humor endlessly to keep the tears at bay. Not a sprout was ever seen. A few months later cement was poured in daisy shapes and painted brilliant colors; the shapes were placed around the hospital grounds. They were hideous and a total waste of time, energy, and money.

The "Vegetable Garden" name stuck with the ward; it was not the preferred place to work. I did manage a six-month stint there and my main memories and lifelong friends were made there. This is truly the place where I grew up.

A third of our patients were put out the back door in body bags to be picked up. The remaining patients were sent home in comas, or paralyzed, partially or fully. It was grim! I think often about the comatose boys; did they wake up, talk, walk, feed themselves, live? We never learned their fate. Is someone still caring for them?

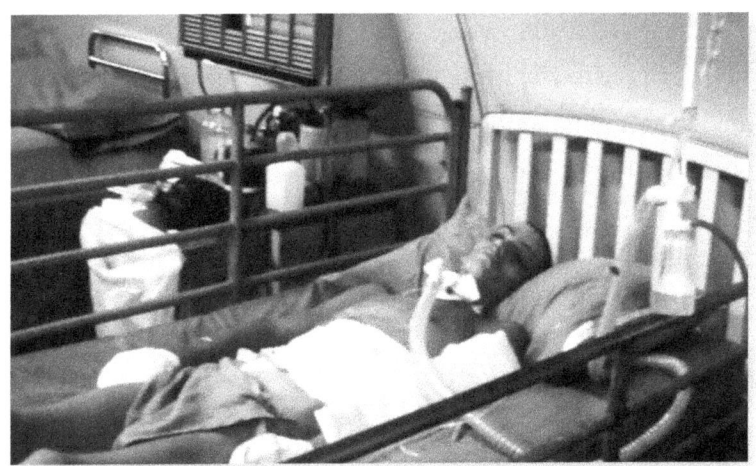
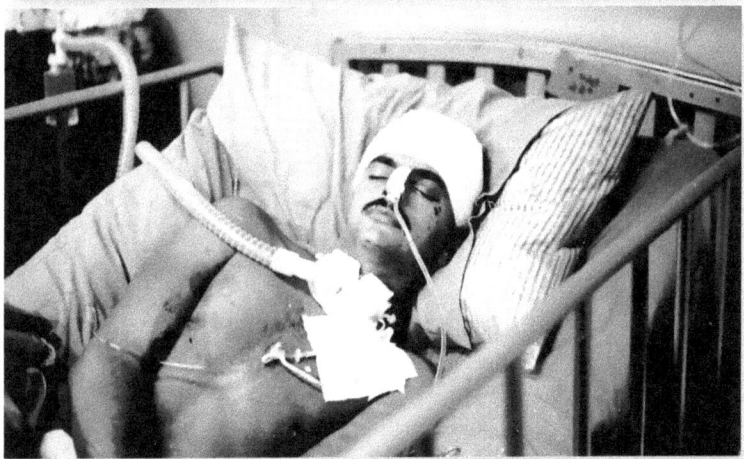
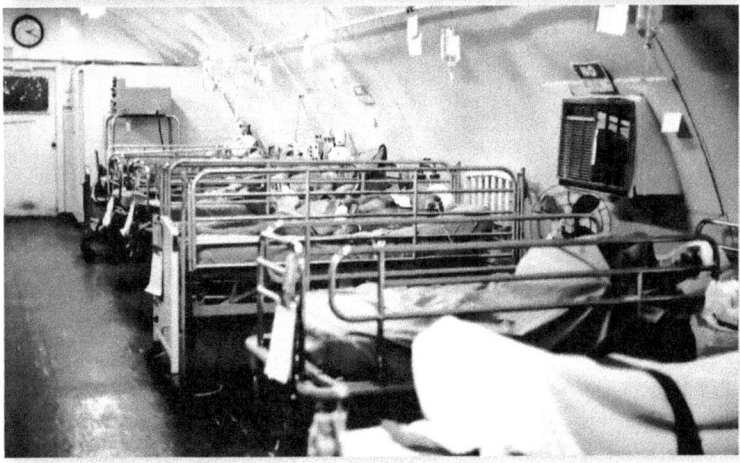

These were fairly typical Ward 5 patients, usually kept only long enough to get them stable, then off they went to a much better equipped hospital in Japan. They usually stayed three days. Some, after surgery, were deemed terminal and we just kept them until they passed.

The paralyzed boys, I knew too well their future, but only in the abstract. The mental, emotional toll for them was huge and it was dumped right on top of their inability to move. A whole new body and lifestyle had to be learned. Who was this new person? How would they manage?

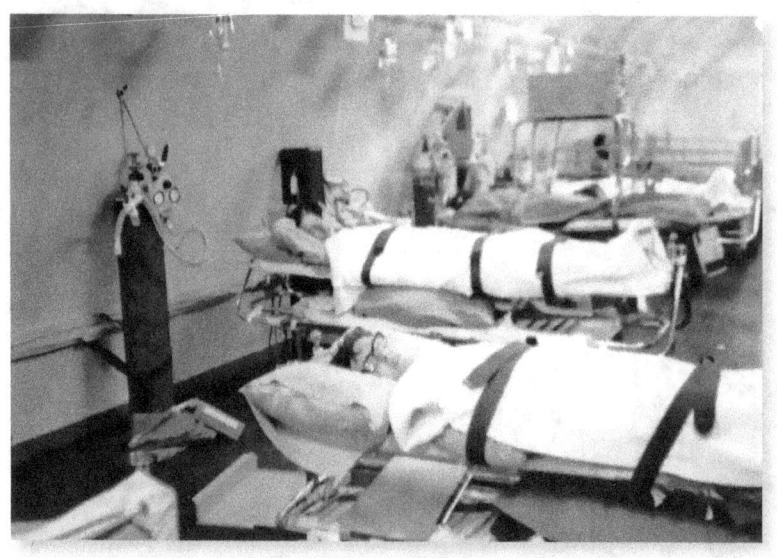

These paralyzed patients are being wrapped up at 4 a.m. to fly out to Japan. Homeward bound, with a hard life ahead.

I learned a lot from Alex, he was one of my patients on Ward 5 that I met up with a few years after the war and we took a four-month van trip through Mexico and Guatemala. It was a wonderful trip, with a wonderful man, a partial quadriplegic. He tried real hard to adjust, but he took his own life on the 20th anniversary of being shot. I often think we should have another wall for all the boys that died *from* Vietnam, not *in* Vietnam.

I will tell you a bit about how we ran this ward. First of all, it was two wards. The less sick had eighteen beds in Ward 6, the very sick and dying had seventeen beds in Ward 5. One nurse and one corpsman ran Ward 6, and two nurses and two corpsmen ran Ward 5. In the Intensive Care section, the beds were lined up heads to the walls; beside each bed was an O_2 tank and a suction machine on a stand. A few tiny windows, a front and back door, and a cement floor completed the scene. There was no privacy; we wanted to see every bed every minute. There was a tiny med and IV room near the back door, and the nurse's desks were in the hallway between the wards, facing their patients. When sitting at your ward desk, you could see all the beds and hear every respirator in your assigned area.

A large bathroom was in the hallway; it was for staff and patients alike, male or female. Supplies were kept on moveable racks in the hallway. This was an extremely organized and efficient system, with very few wasted steps.

The staff worked 12-hour shifts, rotating days and nights every 6 days, with a 36-hour break between rotations so that we got one and a half days off a week. Our tours lasted a year, with people arriving and departing at fairly long intervals, so as not to ruffle the flow of care.

Ward 6 was called the "back pain shammers" ward; how true that was I don't know. I'm sure there might have been a few boys that faked back pain to get out of the fighting, but I will not judge them; they were my patients and all sweethearts to me. Ninety percent were on total bed rest, bored out of their minds, staring at the ceiling. They helped us out, by holding babies, entertaining each other and not complaining too much, although I am sure many were in considerable pain. We also had a few Vietnamese children and adults on that ward with TB of the spine, a grim condition I had not seen before. It was a nice break for us to work on this more cheerful ward.

The corpsmen were the glue that held us together. Mostly 18-year-old draftees, they never wanted to be called enlisted men because they didn't enlist, they were COs — conscientious objectors. We had mostly sweet Midwestern farm boys, hard workers, observant, intelligent, compassionate, and cheerful. They didn't believe in the war, but they took the best care of their patients that was humanly possible, with never a smirk. They needed no reminders; they did their jobs efficiently and always wanted to learn more.

Truth be told, the corpsmen taught us way more than we ever taught them. We were mostly fresh from nursing school, some with tons of book learning and no practical experience. We were in a new world; many procedures were not allowed to be done by nurses in the States and here the corpsman did them with ease. We all caught on fast and helped each other in many ways. The corpsmen took the doctors under their wings also and taught them the ropes.

We were inventive; if they didn't have it in the supply cupboard, we invented it, figured out what worked and passed it on. I will explain a few examples of this.

There is a male incontinence device called a Texas catheter. It is a plastic sheath attached to the penis and the urine drains through a tube into a bag hanging on the bed. No such device was to be found in Vietnam, so we made them out of condoms, tubing and catheter bags, I think we just rubber banded the condom to the tubing. They were changed daily if time allowed, so we needed a lot of them. If anyone had a few minutes, they would assemble a few. One time I noted we were getting low on condoms, so I asked a brand new, very young corpsman to pop over to the Post Exchange to grab a few boxes. I embarrassed the poor sweetheart as he had no idea what a condom was, and I needed to explain. He was so embarrassed; the young and innocent are sent off to war.

Another improvised device was made from an empty plastic gallon bottle that had contained a disinfectant called CIDEX. These bottles were hung over the bed with the bottoms removed, making a funnel for the moist air coming through the tubing inserted in the bottle spout. The oxygen was moistened by bubbling it through water in a bottle, and then it was directed into the patient's airway by the CIDEX funnel. When the doctor wanted the patient to have this treatment, the order was written with one word "CIDEX." In future generations, what might be thought of this cryptic order? Creative improvisations like this worked beautifully and were easy to make.

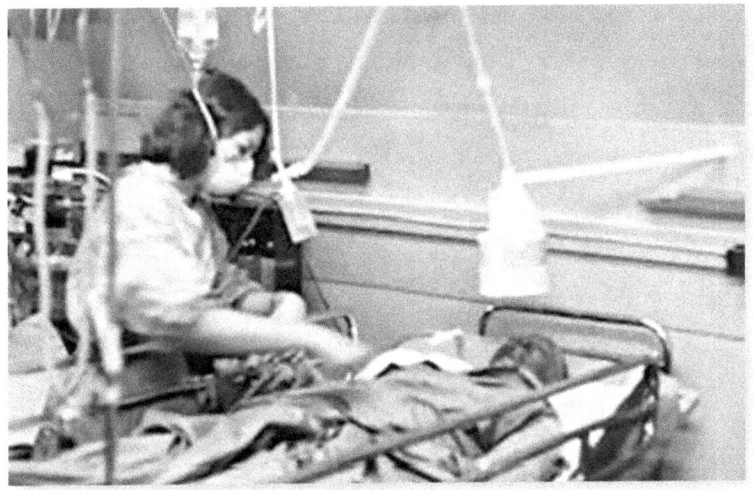

An improvised CIDEX bottle humidifier moistens the oxygen for a civilian patient.

The staff rotated between the two wards, giving people breaks from intensive care. Nurses had one of three jobs. You got Ward 6 alone and when and if you had a break, you went to Ward 5 to help out. On Ward 5 you were either the charge nurse or the med nurse, both were rather grizzly jobs, but the good news was you rarely did either two times running.

The charge nurse oversaw the whole operation, helped the Docs with procedures, checked all the wounds, checked orders, watched over every facet of every patient; mistakes could be deadly. They were in charge of every detail happening on the ward, including all patients, doctors, corpsmen, nurses, therapists and visitors. I can remember roaming my eyes up and down the ward constantly making sure all was as it should be. Your ears were constantly in tune with the respirators. Was there an irregularity in breathing? Where was it and how quick could you get there? Did you make sure the corpsman got a fresh O_2 tank to sit beside the tank in use? The corpsman and IV nurse were listening too, but you were in charge. Most of the Vietnamese patients had a relative present to help with their loved one's care. They were amazingly willing to be helpful to everyone. We would give them little pallets for the floor and situate them around the ward and have them help us listen for irregularities.

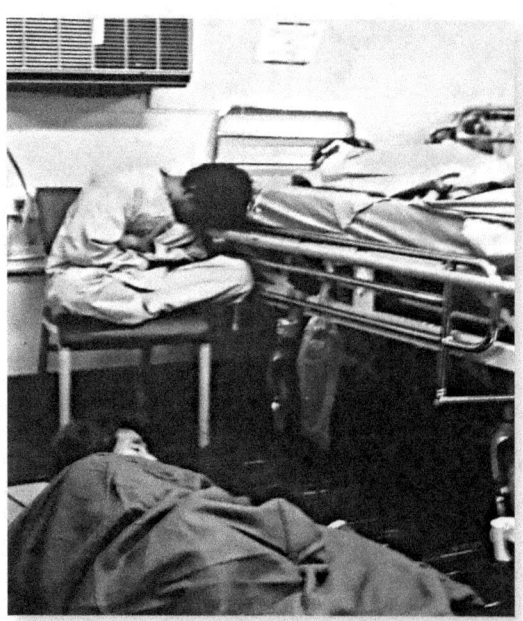

This Vietnamese family is sleeping now, but in the day and if it was a busy night, they would be right up helping us.

By the end of your shift everything done or observed had to be written down, so that we had continuity of care. There was even a formula and order in which it was written so you could find it quickly.

We had an excellent cardex system. Each patient had a section where doctors' orders, nurse notes and vital signs in a graph form were all easily accessible at a glance. You could put this cardex on a cart and roll it around, look at your patient and write descriptions of their conditions, as well as recheck doctor orders and vitals. It was a quick and easy method, no pulling out endless charts and finding the right page, and perhaps missing orders written but not flagged. I loved it; it was so efficient!

The med nurse had a mammoth job, with 17 patients over a 12-hour shift, some with more than one IV. It was a huge number of bottles that needed to be mixed with other solutions; all had to be labeled with what was added, patients name, bed number and what time it was to be hung. Tape, with the hours marked next to milliliters received, was placed on each bottle, so that you could see at a glance if it was running too fast or slow. So, if it was 10 a.m. and your fluids level was at 9 a.m. you had better speed up that IV. Regulating the flow was done by counting drops, something every ICU nurse could and did do in their sleep. The bottle needed to be placed at the bedside before the previous one ran out and if you were lucky someone else would switch them over for you.

Ninety percent of the medicine was given IV or IM (intramuscular) and we found it easier to draw the meds all up at once and place them on trays on top of their medicine cards. Every hour we made the rounds, with our little cart, counting the drops, injecting the meds, checking the IV sites to make sure they stayed intact with thrashing patients. We moved the site of the IV every three days to keep infection at bay. With 17 patients you made continuous loops, never stopping except to reload the cart. I conversed with all my patients; the comatose ones got sweet nothings in their ears and the few awake ones (mostly paralyzed on the Stryker frames) I tried to spend a little time with, reassuring them and trying to get them as comfy as possible on that skinny bed.

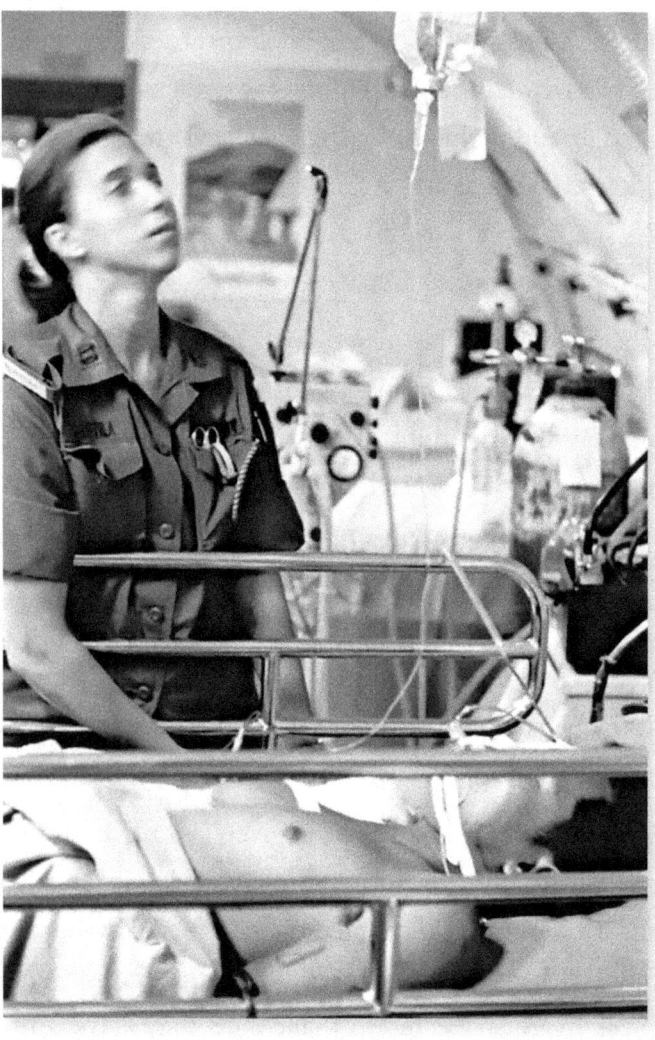

The endless counting of the IV drops.

Once a paralyzed patient thanked me profusely for giving him his shot in his leg where he couldn't feel it. I was shocked, where else would I give it? He told me another nurse said he needed to feel it so it would work better, so he got it in the arm. If I had ever found that nurse, I would have strangled her; didn't that boy have enough on his plate?

The corpsmen were our joy; they found humor in *everything*, and it was contagious. They made most of their work into a game, as fun as possible with no compromise to a patient. Little Mercurochrome gauze strips tied into ribbons would be on the top of every bandaged head in the morning.

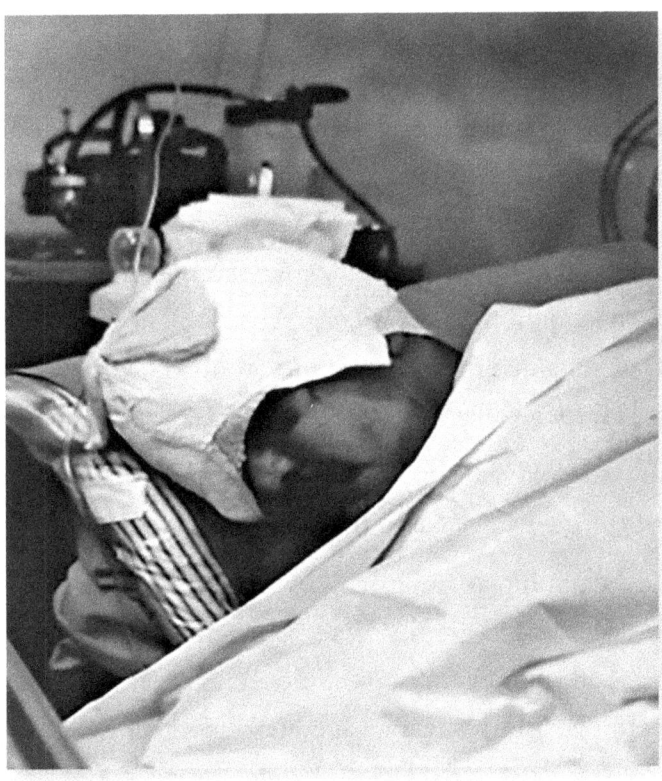

That bow on the head bandage is bright Mercurochrome pink.

Daily baths became fun and all patients were bathed every night. Occasionally patients came to us filthy from the field; this was unusual as they were washed either in the ER or recovery room but when those departments were slammed, they just cleaned the wounded area for surgery, then funneled them on through so the staff could get on to the next patient. They could be really filthy, and I often thought a hose might be nice. The boys of course made a game of it, sometimes declaring it a two- or three-person job assigning each person body parts and racing to get their parts the cleanest, even doing manicures and pedicures. But clean they were and clean they stayed.

Endlessly humping the huge O_2 tanks back and forth to the helipad became fun; who could do it the fastest, who could do the most tanks in a shift? Endless suctioning of tracheostomy and endotracheal tubes became fun. They even named the mucous: the "hawkers" were from the back of the throat, the "lungers" were from much deeper in the chest and went farther with a cough. The corpsmen would even measure how far the sputum would go with a cough. You would hear shouts of, "Wow, look how far that lunger went." They renamed this section of the ward "Hawker Valley" after the song "Harper Valley PTA."

I, being the old lady of 22, just tried to avoid being hit and reminded the guys to clean up the mess.

At the beginning of a shift, it was decided between the two corpsmen who would get the worst job of the day. They were both members of the "emergency bowel movement team" and there were two rolls to play on this team. One lucky member held the patient over and lifted legs and helped change sheets; they also sprayed deodorizer as needed. The unlucky member did the cleanup. The emergency bowel movement cart was quite a sight, fully decorated from *Playboy* magazine and always fully stocked ready for action. I believe the pictures were changed often. Nurses tended to ignore this cart. However, we did pitch in and help with cleanup on occasion, all being part of the team.

The doctors were by and large wonderful, compassionate, thoughtful and kind. They were mostly young and eager to learn. The majority failed the "How to be God" class taught in most medical schools in those days. Humility and tears by the doctors were not strangers on our wards; they made mistakes, as did we all. We comforted each other as best we could when that happened.

We tended to be a little more relaxed on night shift, with only rare doctor visits, few visitors, and more sleeping patients. Just a little less tension, so this is when we played more. Cakes and pizza were cooked up in electric frying pans. We teased and horsed with each other more. Shaving cream battles tended to ensue. Anything to keep the reality of our situation from overwhelming us. One morning I arrived to find the team with colored tape in the form of bikinis taped right over their fatigues. They were on a beach holiday!

Ward 5 had a rhythm, a flow that worked, I think very much due to its excellent staff and head nurse. There was a routine for everything; people knew the order and got in the flow.

One morning I arrived to find all my patients in diapers made with pillowcases. Not the norm and not functional. But the poor night nurse had reached her limit; she said she never wanted to see another penis. I understood her feelings completely but there was no hiding them. We covered our sweet boys with a draw sheet, which is like a half a top sheet. We did our best to keep them covered, but they thrashed and pulled; it was a hard battle we waged and not on the top of our priority list. We needed access to their genitals because they all had internal or external catheters that needed to be kept scrupulously clean and bed sores had to be watched for. They were in comas, not the least bit worried about modesty.

I talk elsewhere in this book about toes; they were always exposed and that's why I touched them as I walked around doing my duties. Human touch can sometimes do wonders. But we also used the toes for a more grim purpose; after a patient had been resuscitated three times, a piece of tape was put around the large right toe which meant to let them go in peace, and note the time of death. I looked for that tape at my arrival for each shift.

I will tell you of three patients that really impacted me on Ward 5.

POSITIVE JOE

Joe was a quadriplegic on a Stryker frame with Crutchfield tongs in place. (They were like ice tongs put in the skull to give traction to the neck to keep things immobilized.) They looked like torture devices, but I don't remember hearing too many complaints about them. Joe happened to be an old boyfriend of one of my nursing school colleagues that went to Vietnam three months before me, and I had actually met him when he was up and walking and not my patient.

Naturally he got special care because I was so horrified to see him there and he was so cheerful and sweet. I mentioned him to my mother in a letter because he lived in a small town where she used to live. She wrote right back and said she remembered him as a baby flirting with her from his highchair, as he spread his oatmeal around. Small world. After the War, he went on to college and law school, had a very successful high-powered career, married and had a family. I have visited him a few times and keep in touch. Where there is a will there is a way and Joe had tons of will. It's been an honor to know him, and I'm glad that I got to have a small part in his care.

THE BOY WITH NO FACE

His head was wrapped in bandages with only his mouth showing. Apparently, the eyes and nose were no longer in existence. He was very young as were they all, he was cognizant and very quiet, never complaining. We were very busy, so he was a bit lost in the shuffle, but I do remember feeding him and myself with a baby on my lap, using the same spoon.

He asked me if he could write a letter home, so I called one of the Red Cross girls to come help him with that. She reported back to me several days later saying the family of this boy had contacted them quite upset. Apparently, the letter was fairly innocuous until the end when he said he couldn't wait to see several family members and friends all of whom were dead. We hadn't even seen that horrendous depression but of course it was there, as it was with so many of them.

LOUIE THE HEARTBREAKER

Louie was one of our few awake head injury patients; he had fallen off the back of a truck. Luckily after a few days he seemed fine, but not fit for duty quite yet. So he was being sent home to the States. I remember the morning well; he was so excited, joy radiated through him and latched on to us. It was so rare to send home someone awake and functioning. I was the charge nurse, so I was getting him ready to leave, paperwork and an exam. I was horrified when he told me he had watery discharge from one nostril. Seems simple, right, just a little cold. Not so; every fiber in my neurosurgical intensive care nursing mind stood up and screamed. This was not nasal discharge but cerebral spinal fluid from the brain.

Instead of going home that day Louie went into surgery. The outcome was grim; he had a crack in his cribriform plate which in the early 1970's was not as easily treated as now. He returned to us in rough shape, and I don't remember all the details and complications, but I do know he developed diabetes insipidus and seizures. He was still awake and communicating with us and we were falling more and more in love with him. After a time, we knew that death was inevitable and he went into a coma, but we gave it one last try. The neurosurgeon decided to send him to a better hospital in Japan; he and one of my dear nurse friends went with him. They even padded the helicopter when he left to prevent more seizures. He died within a day or two after arrival. It was a particularly rough death for all of us; to go from such joy to such frustration and failure was hard to bear.

CHAPTER 3

THE BABIES

The first patient I met in Vietnam oddly enough was a baby; she was two months old, named Le Thi Kim Phuong. It was my first day in country, and I was having a tour of the 24th Evac Hospital in Long Binh. After the tour, I was assigned to Ward 5 Neurosurgical Intensive Care, right where that baby was. We called her Lee Ahn; I would take care of her (sometimes from afar) for the next year. She brought great joy to this grim ward, where 90% of the patients were comatose, in dementia or permanently paralyzed. Lee Ahn was our little spark of light, fat cheeked and smiley. She had been thrown in a garbage can as a newborn, landing on her head — all because she was half black, not acceptable in that society. Conceived no doubt from desperation to earn money to feed the other children, or through violence, or perhaps a little tryst.

The GI's often lied to these girls, promising marriage and a future in the States. One of the married doctors actually had an apartment in Saigon to keep his girlfriends. You literally had to walk over the boxes of condoms in order to get in and out of the Post Exchange. The Army was worried about venereal diseases; I was worried about babies.

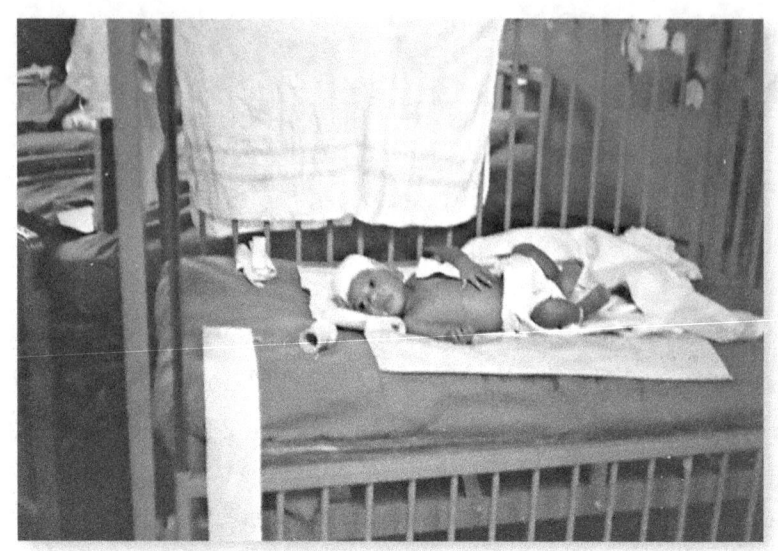

Lee Thi Kim Phoung (Lee Ahn) when I first arrived.

Lee Ahn on the back porch with a new friend.

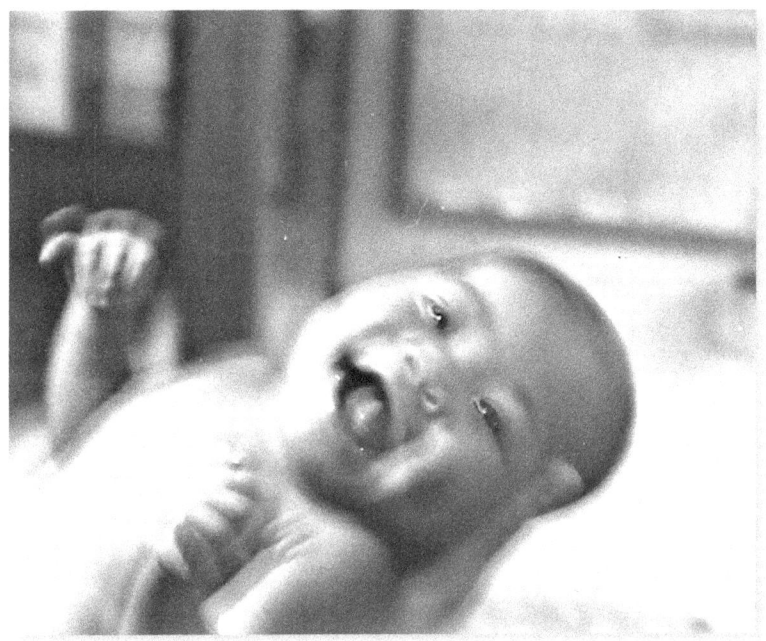

Lee Ahn with her sunny smile.

Many newborns in Vietnam during the war died in their first year. Food, housing, time and energy were in short supply. I have always said that babies and children are always the biggest losers in a war.

We had few baby supplies at the hospital, but for some reason we happily had a few cribs and some baby bottles. We used big wound bandages for diapers, taped on. Stretchy knit cotton tubing that was used under plaster casts made great little outfits and hats.

Lee Ahn was loved by all. She had a sunny disposition and was a quiet baby, both handy features on a busy, busy ward. She was picked up as often as possible and occasionally handed to one of the patients on Ward 6, which was part of the Neuro ward, but for people with minor back injuries. These poor guys were admitted and put on bed rest in a firm flat bed and were so bored; they were happy to exchange smiles with a baby.

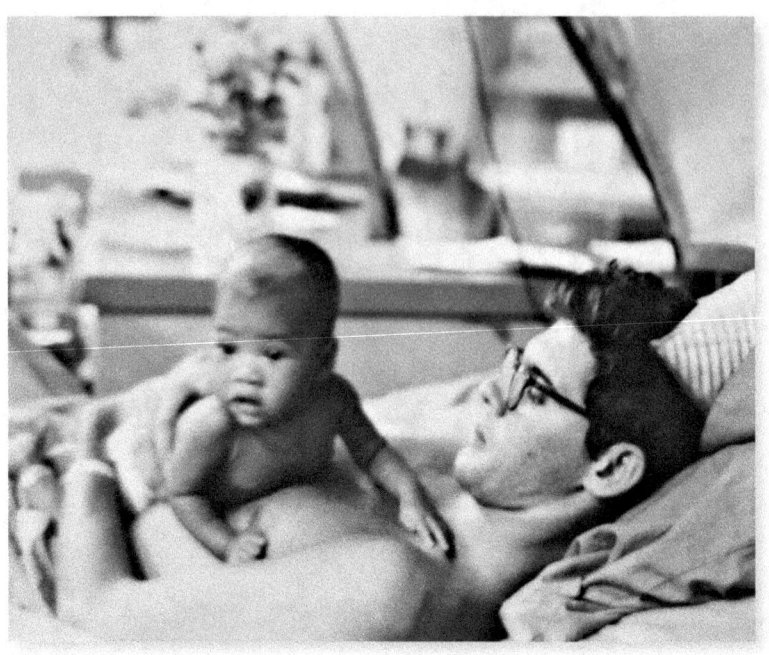

Lee Ahn trying to alleviate the boredom on Ward 6.

I mostly remember, holding that little sweetheart while I ate. We could go to the Mess Hall, but I usually chose to grab a tray of food. No plates, just a compartmented tray; I'd add Lee Ahn's food to the tray and then find a patient that needed to be fed. I'd sit on his bed, baby on my lap and feed us all, often using the same spoon; a quick and efficient method that I think the GI's enjoyed the most.

Well, Lee Ahn was a sick little baby. After I'd been there a month, she became a little lethargic and it was determined that she was developing hydrocephalus, commonly known as "water on the brain." They can put a needle in the fontanel (the soft spot on top of the head) to drain the excess fluid, and it gives temporary relief. The Docs said if we didn't find a shunt — which was a tiny piece of tubing that just allowed fluid to drain in one direction, we would lose our baby.

There were no shunts at any facilities in Vietnam. I asked the Doc to write down exactly what he needed. I had already signed up to make a phone call stateside. Within hours I was talking to my mother (aka Wonder Woman). The story was told, and she was on it, on the phone for 24 hours, and that tube was in our hands within 48 hours. It was free, exactly what we needed, and sent with a loving note from the factory. My father used to say that when my mother heard a fire bell, she was always the first one out the door to help anyone she could. She never failed me — a terrific, powerful woman.

Time passed; Lee Ahn grew and got better and was sent to the local orphanage. Yikes! I was upset! I had been to that orphanage in Bien Hoa; not good! It was packed with babies. I hate to even think what the mortality rate must have been.

The babies at this orphanage lay three to a tiny crib on a metal mesh surface. Bottles of questionable cleanliness and contents were propped, babies sucking the best they could with clogged or torn nipples, causing them to choke as the contents poured into their mouths. Other older babies just lay under the cribs on the tile floors with the urine and milk trickling down on them. The nuns fluttered around, all immaculate and well fed with diamond rings on their fingers. To be fair, I never talked to them except to get a baby's name, so I'm not sure exactly what was going on, but I was certainly never comfortable there.

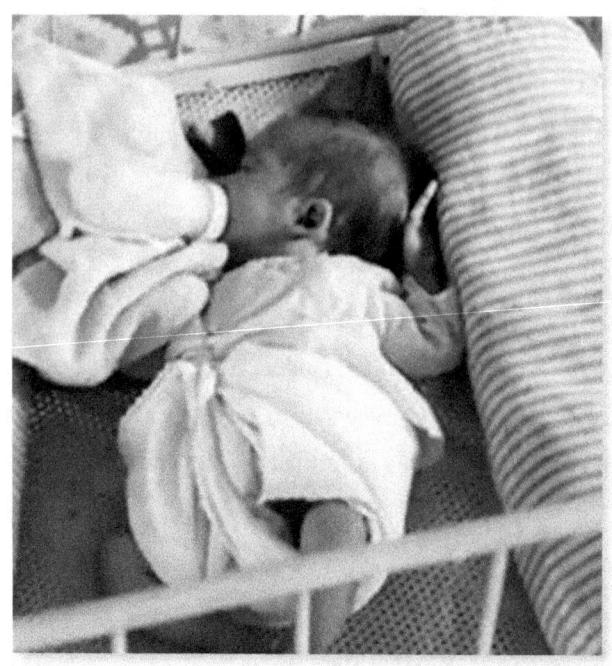

Babies lying three to a bed on metal mesh with a propped bottle.

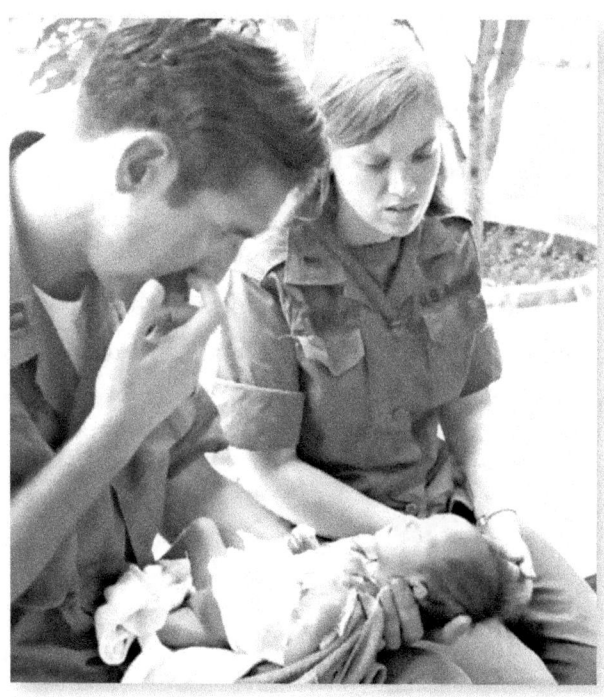

Baby being inspected by the team at the Bien Hoa orphanage; this little one didn't make it.

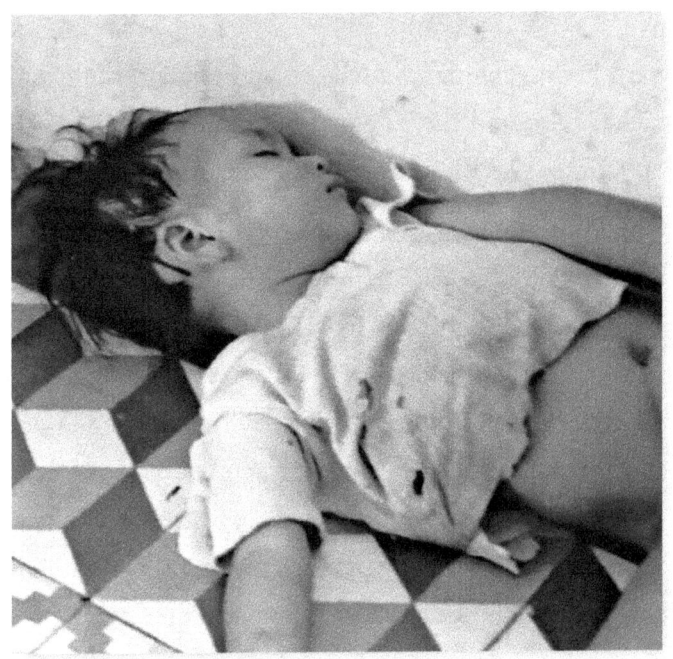

The older babies lay on the floor at Bien Hoa orphanage.

The author holding an unhappy baby from the Bien Hoa orphanage.

Our ward had a jeep named Mighty Ralph, and the hospital had a pediatrician, who had the title of Public Health Officer. We often made jeep trips to the Bien Hoa orphanage.

The human toll of the war was a relentless agony for us, but at the orphanages we could at least help some of the children get a better start. Left untreated, babies who were born with birth defects or operable injuries would most likely die, slowly, of malnutrition. At the 24th Evac Hospital we could deal with things like correcting cleft lips, cleft palates, clubbed feet, fractures, and infections, and we loved doing it. Furthermore, our docs were mostly young and inexperienced, and needed to practice what they would be doing stateside. So, when the wards were slow, the docs would comb the orphanages and Vietnamese hospitals looking for people to help.

Trips to the Bien Hoa orphanage usually resulted in us bringing back more than one sick little one. The surgical cases usually did quite well, with cleft lips repaired and club feet straightened. We usually kept them for many months. We got quite fond of them, and some wormed their way solidly into a staff member's heart and got taken back to the U.S.

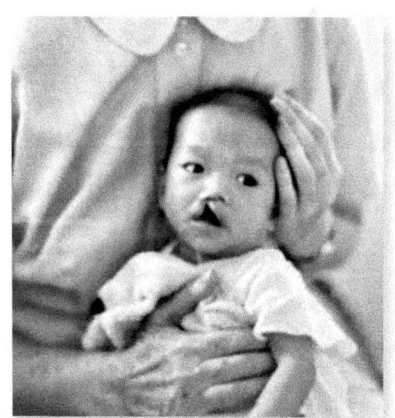
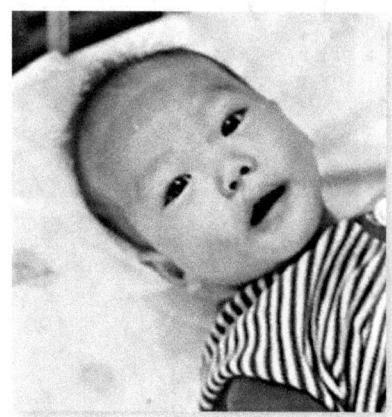

A beautiful cleft lip repair.

The medical cases didn't always fare so well. The death rate was high and the cost to our already breaking hearts was hard to bear. Once a dear doctor friend woke me mid-day because one of the babies he had been doctoring for quite a while had died. He needed a good long cry in my arms so he could get back to work.

We started looking for babies slightly healthier, that had a better chance of living, hoping to keep our morale up. That seems so harsh to even say, but that was my Vietnam. There was never enough time, energy or equipment, just endless frustration and longing to do more, and never finishing my job. On several occasions, I tied a baby to my chest and carried it with me as I worked, stroking that little head and talking to it, as it slowly died. The babies needed a respirator, which we didn't have, and I would not let them die alone in their beds. I occasionally took a baby back to my hooch at night to care for it, especially if the ward was swamped or the nurse on duty disliked Vietnamese or babies.

So, since the orphanage we got these little guys from was so wretched, we had a real hard time taking them back there at discharge. I came up with two solutions, one was to find them homes in the States; after all, most of them were half American; and the other was to find a better orphanage.

We had one day off a week, so early on in my tour of Vietnam, I grabbed a corpsman and we went to Saigon, about 40 minutes down the road. I always traveled with a corpsman to protect me from the GI's, and they liked to go with a nurse to protect them from the "tea ladies." We helped each other out against the robbers and beggars, mostly children. Tricky, aggressive, little buggers that broke your heart.

The author holding a respirator baby as it died. We are both in pajama tops.

Over many weeks we found several good orphanages and a terrific Seventh Day Adventist Hospital. I made arrangements for our babies to be taken in when needed. Next, I took pictures of babies, and those pictures were stuffed in my pockets and shown to every GI I ever met, along with explanations on how to adopt. I even helped with the paperwork. Only six went home to new families, but they had a chance for a better life.

The author taking a little one to Saigon for adoption paperwork.

Lots of the little ones, including Lee Ahn, got to go to an orphanage run by a woman whose husband worked at the U.S. embassy. I remember neither the name of the woman or her business, but in my mind she was an "angel." She worked alone, training local women; the babies got excellent care and she got many adopted. Our Lee Ahn was kind of "removed" from the awful orphanage and slipped in there with the Angel. Unfortunately, due to her head injuries and frequent uncontrollable seizures, causing developmental delays, she likely was never adopted and probably died young. Hopefully she is at peace; her fat cheeks and smiles did a beautiful job soothing nurses and patients alike on Wards 5 and 6.

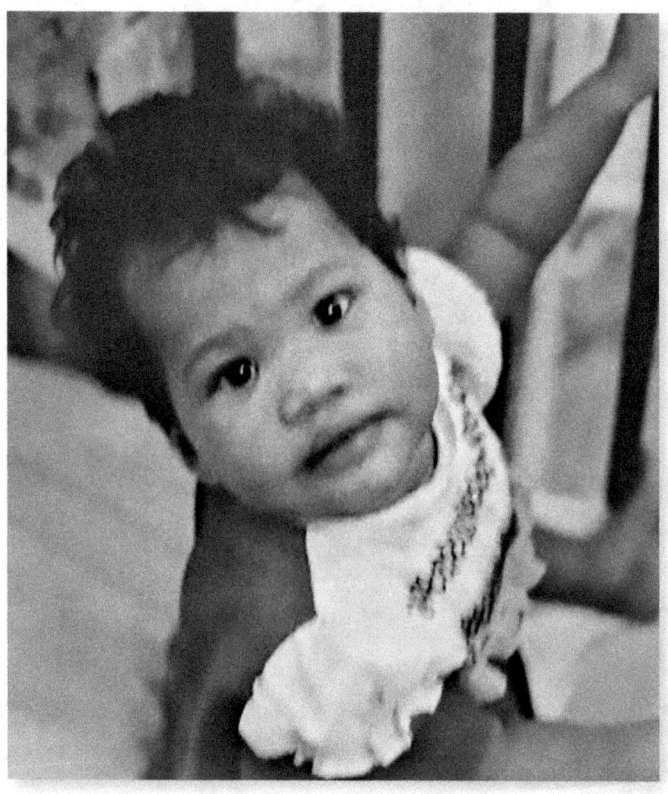

Lee Ahn at the Angel orphanage.

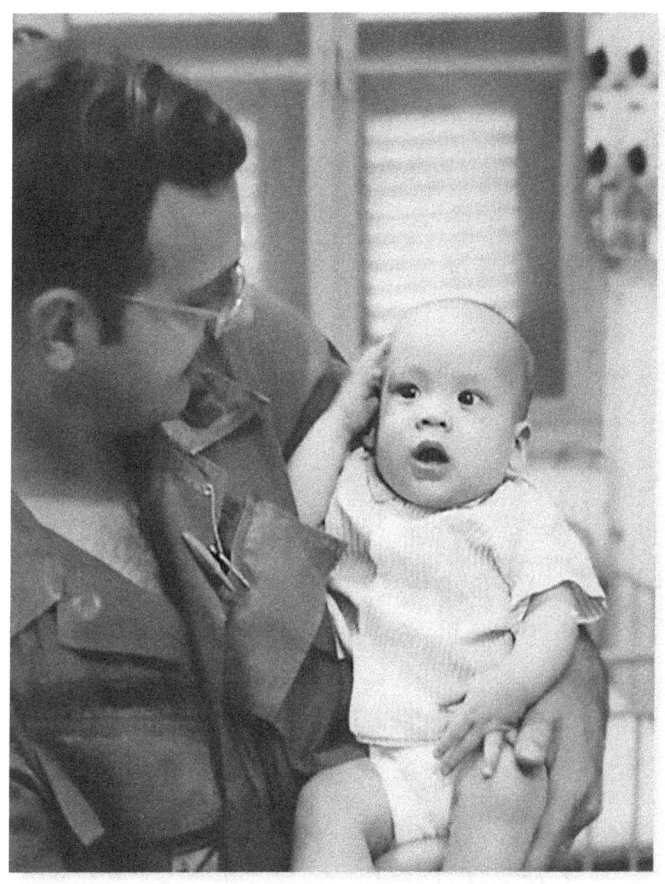

Prospective father and a beautiful half American boy.

Lee Ahn's new orphanage got lots of visits from me, where I often brought potential fathers in to adopt. I got close to the nameless Angel running the nursery, and like everyone living in a country at war, she was short on supplies. She had incubators, but no infant feeding tubes. Some surgical instruments were lacking and there were no oxygen tanks. I am my mother's daughter and jumped right to the task.

Back on base, I had heard about corpsmen stealing instruments and selling them on the black market. I believe there was a bit of a surplus because a hospital had closed, but I was still horrified. I had never stolen anything in my life. I reclassified this in my head as saving lives, not thievery. It wasn't hard to do; we were winding down, and we had plenty of supplies. I took the needed instruments and the newborn feeding tubes. Oddly enough, I found a box of those feeding tubes that had never been opened in a supply cupboard; undoubtedly, they had been sent over by accident.

The oxygen tanks would be quite a bit trickier. I had a corpsman scout out the situation and he reported an overabundance of tanks, so I had no qualms about taking a few. The problem was the giant size and weight of the big green beasts, especially since I wanted them full and heavier. I could barely move them with a dolly myself.

I needed a corpsman to come to the rescue. We had lots of them; they adored the nurses, and the feeling was mutual. I found someone on my same schedule and let him in on the plan. He had no hesitation; he was in. I decided to jump in with two feet and trust to luck and the power of the round-eyed girl, that was me. Most of the guys would do anything for a nurse.

I sent my corpsman to grab the tanks right after shift at 7 a.m. and bring them to the back stoop of the ward. We would hitchhike from there. Someone was watching over me, as the first vehicle to go by was an ambulance with a helpful driver. He was thrilled to take us and the tanks to the Cholon districts in Saigon. The tanks were being appropriated — no problem. It would take three hours out of his day — no problem. It was so handy to have the tanks in an ambulance; who would ever notice? The thanks and hugs received when we got to the orphanage made the ambulance driver feel like a hero. Several months later, I saw the tanks; they had been transformed. The Angel lady said they needed refilling, which had to be done at the Army hospital. She couldn't let them think that she had stolen them, so she knitted them both huge form-fitting sweaters to wear; they were now pink and pretty, with unquestionable ownership.

I got the *Fairbanks Daily News-Miner*, weekly, sent by a friend. It said that the Americans were not in Cambodia. Well, then how did I have this adorable Cambodian six-year-old boy named Chow Rhim on my ward? He was all alone and had a frag wound on his head; he was with us for many, many months.

Chow Rihm the day he left to go home to Cambodia.

Chow Rihm entertaining a corpsman.

The majority of our civilian Vietnamese patients had a family member who stayed to help care for their loved one: they willingly helped us with every task we gave them and volunteered for more. They were terrific. We all felt so sorry for this little squirt, swooped up and helicoptered in before a family member could join him.

So, of course we gathered him right in and did our best as substitute parents. Miraculously, several months after his arrival, Chow Rhim's grandpa arrived on the ward! He had walked and hitched rides all the way from Cambodia. He was a wonderful kind man; I think we were all as happy to see him as Chow Rhim was. After Grandpa's arrival, our little patient began to thrive.

Chow Rhim's Grandpa came all the way from Cambodia.

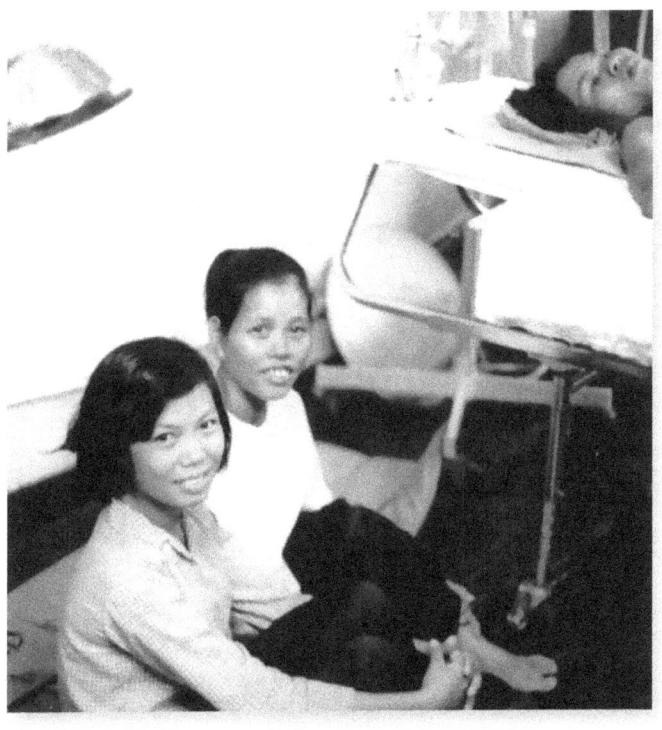

Family members were always ready to help.

We had many children and babies with frag wounds. I can't tell all their stories, but they all have a little place in my heart, as do their parents who never left their sides.

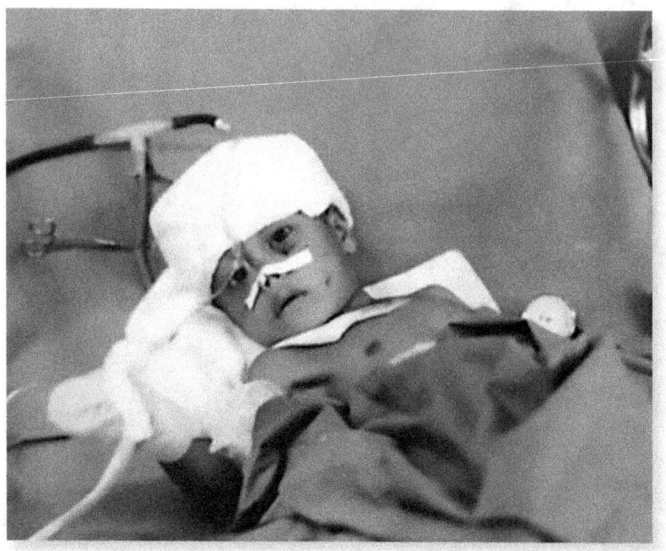

Someone stepped on a mine; this little guy was in the wrong place.

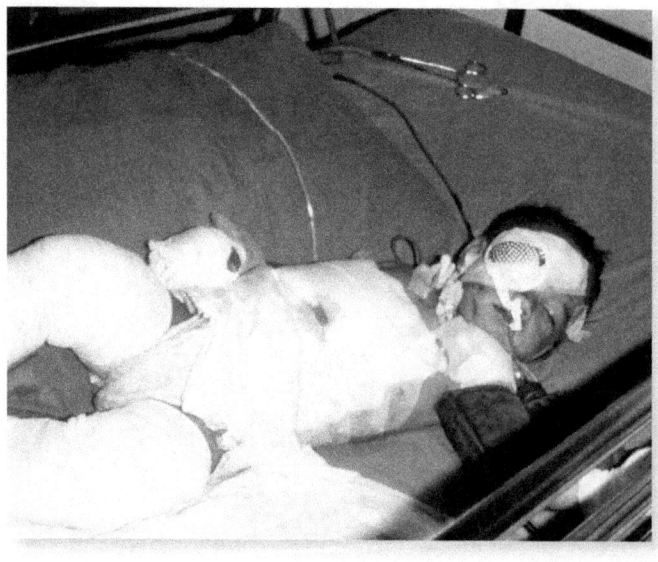

This little fellow did fairly well.

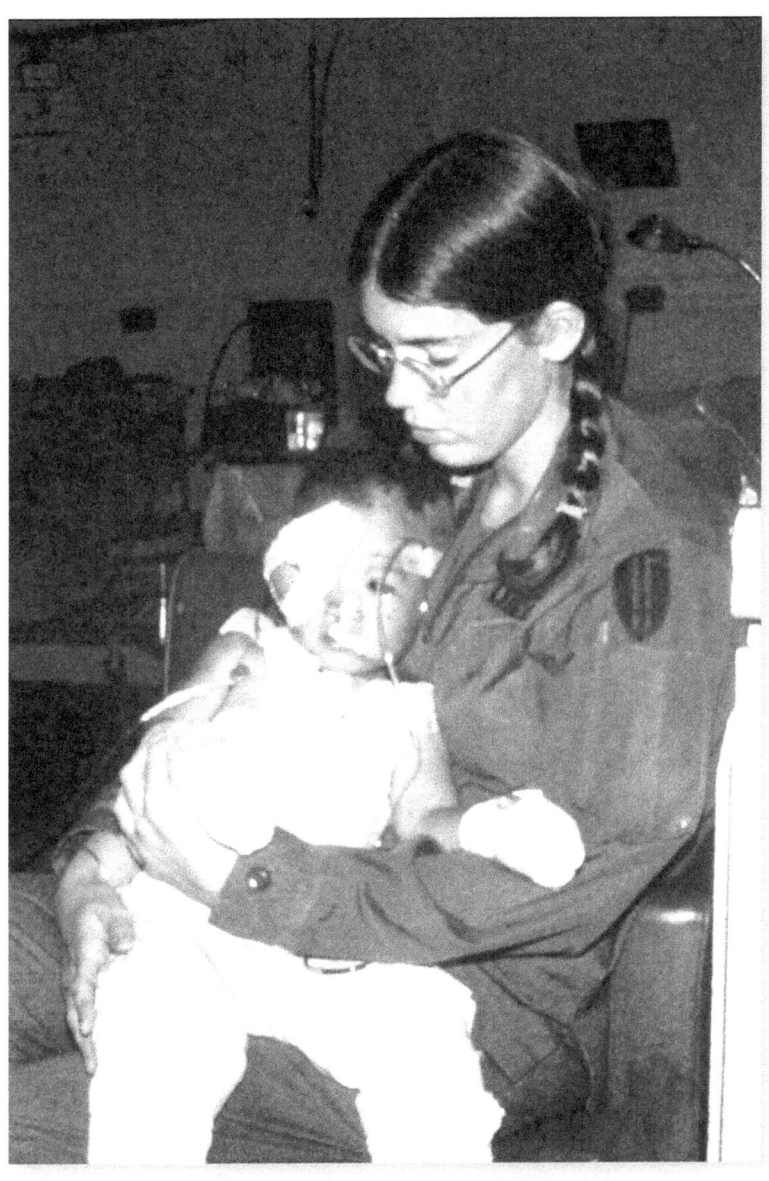

A fellow just needs a hug in the middle of the night
and he found a spot on the author's lap.

One mother especially tore my heart open. She was older than many of the mothers, and for a bit, I thought that she might be the grandmother of the infant she was holding in the bed, but then I saw the baby at her breast and knew the truth. The baby had a head injury and had had head surgery; no more could be done, so we waited and watched. She was an excellent mother, and we were extremely busy, so we just let her tend the baby. One morning I came on shift, and I saw tears in her eyes; the report told me the baby was dying. I went to her, to offer comfort, one of our Vietnamese aides that spoke a bit of English by my side. She began to wail and said that she wanted to die, too, as this was the 14th child she had lost, some to disease but most of them to this horrible, senseless, idiotic war.

A BABY STORY IN PICTURES

I am holding Nguyen Van Tung — immediately nick-named Tongue Blade. I am wetting him down, as his temperature is 105° F. We are at the unfortunate Bien Hoa Orphanage.

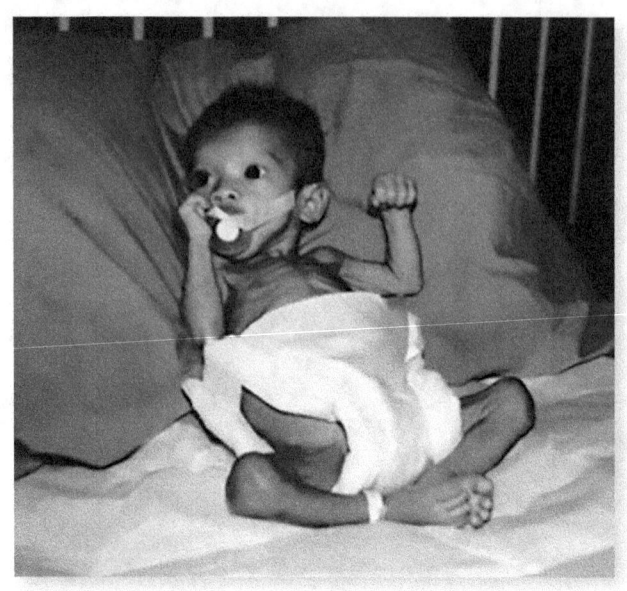

The next day at the 24th Evac Hospital, he is much happier.

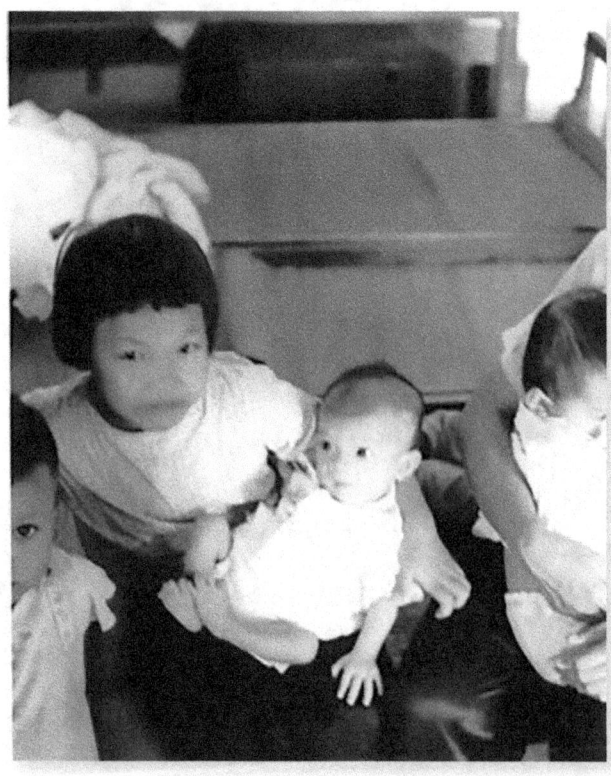

Return to the Bien Hoa orphanage.

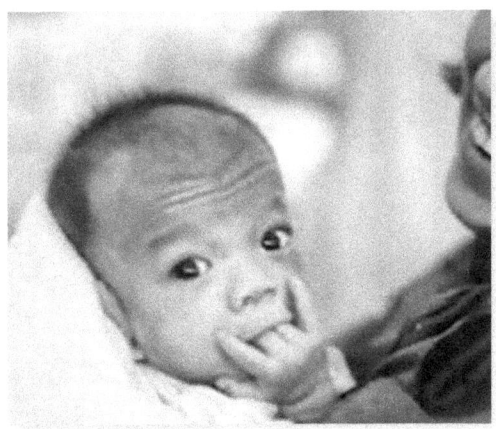

Mr. Tongue Blade, by now a favorite of the ward and completely healthy being returned to the Bien Hoa orphanage. Our hearts were breaking.

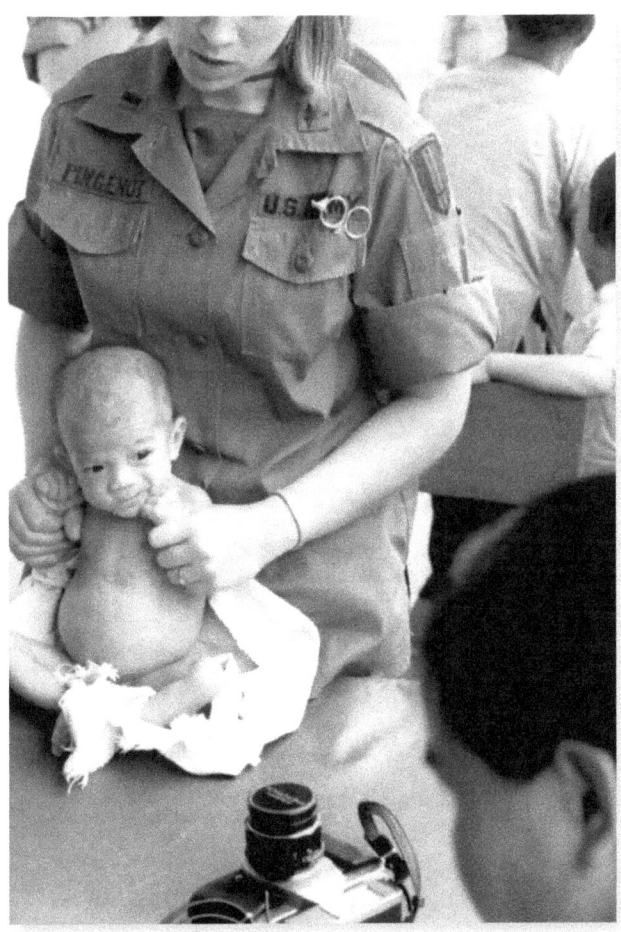

This is one week later; he was in rough shape, and so we brought him back to the 24th Evac Hospital.

On the right is dear Tongue Blade, slipped into the lovely Angel orphanage after another little stay with us at the 24th Evac. A happy little story in grim times. We hope that he is having a happy life.

CHAPTER 4

WARDS 2 AND 3

After Ward 5, I was transferred to Wards 2 and 3 Intensive Care with a burn unit and a general surgical ward. I was hoping, by asking for a transfer, to have a lighter load to carry. I'm not sure that it was the least bit lighter, but now I had far more awake patients that I could interact with, and fall more in love with, before they died. I could actually look into their eyes and talk to them. We did have a lower mortality rate, but we also had fewer patients with the war winding down, but aside from the Burn Unit, it was generally easier. It didn't seem to run quite as efficiently as Ward 5, but the patients still got excellent care.

Two patients stand out in my mind from the ICU Ward 2. One was Kevin and his final kiss, and the other was a Thai soldier. I don't remember his name; I met him and deathed him in a matter of hours. He of course was young and sweet and smiley as were most of the Thais. He was brought to us from the recovery room. His injuries were extensive, but he was awake and talking. He had suffered a massive blood loss and been given countless bottles of blood, which caused a condition where the blood would no longer clot. We were told by the surgeon that they had done everything possible, and he would bleed to death and didn't have long to go. I immediately called for a Thai interpreter; this boy certainly needed to know what was happening. The interpreter left and the boy looked so shocked. I have noted that most 18-year-old boys think they are invincible. This boy was no different and this was a heck of a lot to process in a very short time. I stood with him holding his hand caressing his hair for a while until he was gone, my pants and boots and the floor filling with his blood.

The general surgical Ward 3 allowed me to watch those beautiful boys heal from their minor wounds so they could be sent back to the fighting. There were also general minor surgeries like hernia repairs, appendectomies and circumcisions. It also gave me a whole group of soldiers that were eager to talk and get to know and that were mostly mobile. There was lots of horsing around and joking on this ward.

What we appreciated most was their mobility and wanting to please the nurses and help us out. They were great for running errands, like taking specimens to the lab, getting snacks from the mess hall, or delivering papers. They helped us hold down patients and did reading and writing for them. Not only did this help us, it helped them: it took their minds off their future and their pain. It was hard for them to complain about their tiny wounds when they were helping us with a critical patient. We all loved the interaction.

One job the corpsmen had that was particularly grizzly, which I tended to try and avoid, was the daily wound cleaning. All frag wounds were debrided (cleaned and smoothed out, ready for suturing) in the OR (operating room). The wounds were left open and covered with gauze and the patient sent to the ward. There the wound was irrigated twice daily with saline and hydrogen peroxide. If the wounds were extensive or particularly deep, pain meds were given for the procedure. If not too severe, they were just cleaned quickly and efficiently. Meds or not, it was always very painful. On the third day the corpsmen sutured the wounds with stainless steel wire, which they didn't have to tie, as it could be simply twisted. These wounds did very well with rarely an infection. The larger wounds were taken back to the operating room for more refined stitchery.

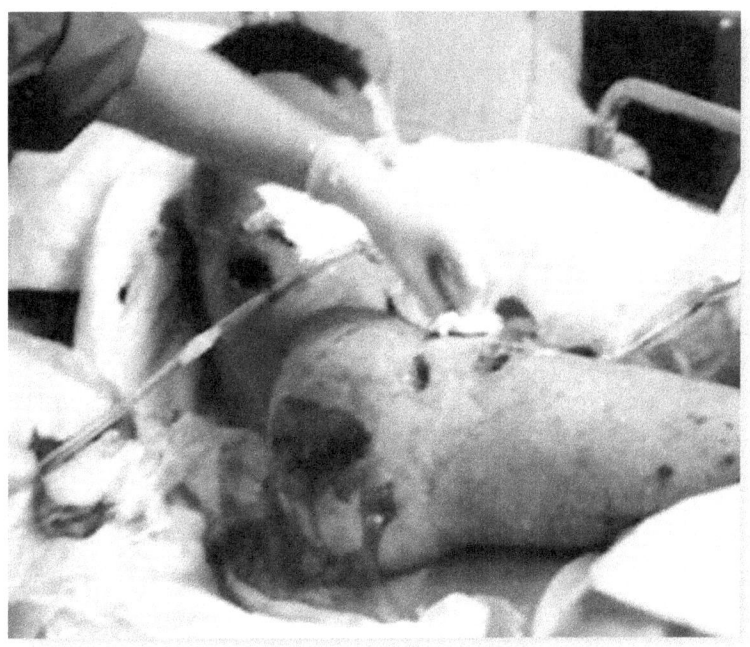

Multiple frag wounds are being cleaned.

I spent five months or so on these wards and Ward 3 was a treat, especially after a stint in the ICU or the Burn Unit. There wasn't as much continuity on the wards at this time, as we had fewer patients and the corpsmen tended to be shifted from one ward to another.

One night I had an unfamiliar corpsman. Shifts were far easier when you had the old regulars that you knew and trusted. There were not tons of things to do on a ward like this at night, as most of the guys just slept, and I would wander over to the ICU and give them a hand, leaving the corpsman to get me if there was a problem. Well, this night I made the rounds and tucked everyone in and all was quiet. I went looking for my corpsman because I hadn't seen him in a long time, and I wanted to go help next door. I also wanted to see his 8 p.m. vital signs and get them quickly charted. I looked everywhere, asked all the staff on the ICU. All the awake patients were queried, and I soon discovered that vitals hadn't been taken.

Now I was worried, I didn't know this kid, or his habits or routine, but I did know that he had to tell me if he was leaving or couldn't do his job. I finally thought to look in the bathroom; perhaps he was sick?

I found him in a stall, passed out with a needle in his arm. His vitals were OK, so I got the corpsman from Ward 2 and put him to bed. I now had another patient, and the ward to myself.

This boy was a different kind of victim of the war, but I didn't see much of that side of things since I only worked the surgical wards. I did, however, see the marijuana side, as it was absolutely everywhere. I only smoked it second hand, as it was at every party and hard to avoid; I just felt I needed to be at my best to do my job. Many did avoid it and quite a few indulged, but I never saw a problem on the wards with performance, and I never felt it to be a big issue. Perhaps I was just naive and it was a way bigger issue in the field.

CHAPTER 5

THE BURN UNIT

I hated it! We all did: a grim, fairly hopeless place, only four beds, almost always full. Swollen, bloated bodies, thankfully mostly in comas, hardly recognizable as people. We slogged through our 12-hour shifts, only one nurse in there, alone, exhausted, frustrated, sad. I don't remember ever sitting during the 12-hour shift. I ate, took notes, and did every procedure standing, hurrying to get to the next task; they were endless; we never finished, just handed them off to the next nurse and dragged ourselves to bed, so we could return in twelve hours. Luckily we rarely had more than three shifts in a row. I'm sure we would have broken down otherwise.

The Burn Unit was given to us when the 93rd Evac Hospital closed in April 1971, as the war was winding down. I only worked there off and on for three months. During that time, we had a 100% mortality rate.

I know a lot of you have heard of napalm, a jellied gasoline used extensively in Vietnam, which burned and tortured its victims. Fortunately, I never saw its results. I also never took care of an American GI in this unit. We had French and American civilians in house fires, but mostly we had what we called "shit burners." These were young Vietnamese men who had the awful job of pulling out half barrels of human waste from the backs of the outhouses, dousing them with gasoline and setting them on fire. I'm sure they got very few or any lessons on the dangers of gasoline, as we had way too many casualties; it seemed so useless.

The first thing you worry about with a burn patient is an airway. Having all my patients coming from the recovery room or the ER, that problem was taken care of for me: most of the patients were intubated and on a respirator. The second worry is the fluid-electrolyte balance. Burns swell, the water is drawn from the body core and put in the external tissues; this causes dehydration. The third worry is infection. Those second two worries took up every minute of my 12-hour shift, but I must admit the water-electrolyte imbalance killed most of my patients and utterly exhausted me.

With four patients I had only fifteen minutes per hour for each. First, I had to check the vital signs, which included a pulse in all four extremities to be sure the swelling was not cutting off circulation, causing gangrene.

Intake and output was my nightmare, and that came next. The IV fluids came in glass 1-liter bottles. The bottles were marked with milliliters on the side and the patient got so many milliliters an hour, according to their output. You measured milliliters to see how many drops an hour were administered. To know how many drops were going in, the drops had to be counted and regulated with a sliding clamp on the tubing. X number of drops equaled X number of milliliters administered and this varied with the type of tubing used, be it pediatric or adult. To give us an added check, we would put tape next to the numbers on the bottles and mark them with the hours. So, if your level of liquid matched where it should be at a certain hour, you were on the mark and could tell at a glance.

To know how much fluid to give, you had to know how much had been lost, something impossible to measure accurately. The urine was measured, and specific gravity determined to know the concentration. What about the loss from the skin, lungs, stomach, bowels? That loss had to be estimated (mostly guessed) in order to calculate how much liquid should be given over the next hour.

Next, we had to suction the trach tube. Then came the turning, a job best suited for two caregivers. We had a top sheet folded in half underneath and crossways on the bed, shoulders to thighs. We could grab the tail on that sheet and pull them towards us, so we had room on the bed to get them on their sides. Then we raised the bed rails to keep them off the floor and raced around to the other side of the bed, grabbed that same sheet tail and rolled them like a burrito onto their sides, quickly checking the cleanliness and skin integrity on the side now exposed. Next, pillows were stuffed behind them to hold them in place. Quickly, thanking the universe that they were clean with all unburned skin intact, you moved on to the burn cream, replacing it when necessary, and picking off any dead skin with your gloved hand. That dead stuff was a great breeding ground for infection. These all seemed like useless tasks to me because nickel-sized spiders loved that burn cream and I can't begin to tell you how many of them I pulled off my patients daily. Was I getting their fluids in balance just so they could die from infection deposited by the spiders?

I'm pretty sure I *never* got all those tasks done in fifteen minutes, but I just moved on to the next patient as fast as possible and hoped for no interruptions.

Unwary doctors came in occasionally, and I allowed them to see their patients and write orders, but I never let them escape without helping with turning, spider and skin picking, and my *favorite* — fluid balancing. I swear I spent my whole year in Vietnam counting drops in my sleep, but never more than in that Burn Unit!

One shift, I arrived, and to my delight we had an awake patient. He was a Vietnamese civilian named Huy with only a few burns above his waist, so his airway was fine, and he could move himself around the bed a bit. He was a sweet man but knew not a word of English. My Vietnamese consisted of four words starting with "p": pain, pee, pooh, and pretty. Useful words for sure but not great for conversation starters. So we flapped our hands at each other and smiled and got by OK. He was so scared, and I was at a loss with how to help him. Thinking on it all these years later, I should have found an interpreter. He did luck out though with having only two roommates instead of three, so I had a tiny bit more time. His legs and feet were burned almost to the bone in places, and we cut the skin hip to toe on both legs to allow for expansion; this procedure is called an escharotomy. Huy's legs didn't hurt because the nerve endings were destroyed, but the lesser burns on his arms were giving him excruciating pain. I comforted him as best I could, with drugs, soft talking, hand touching: there is a universal language of love.

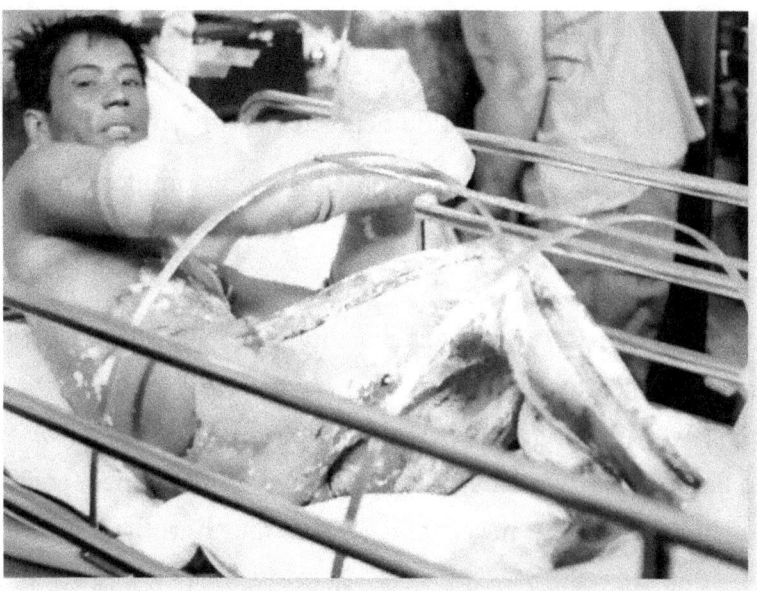

Huy newly arrived; the skin on his legs has been cut lengthwise to allow for tissue swelling — an escharotomy.

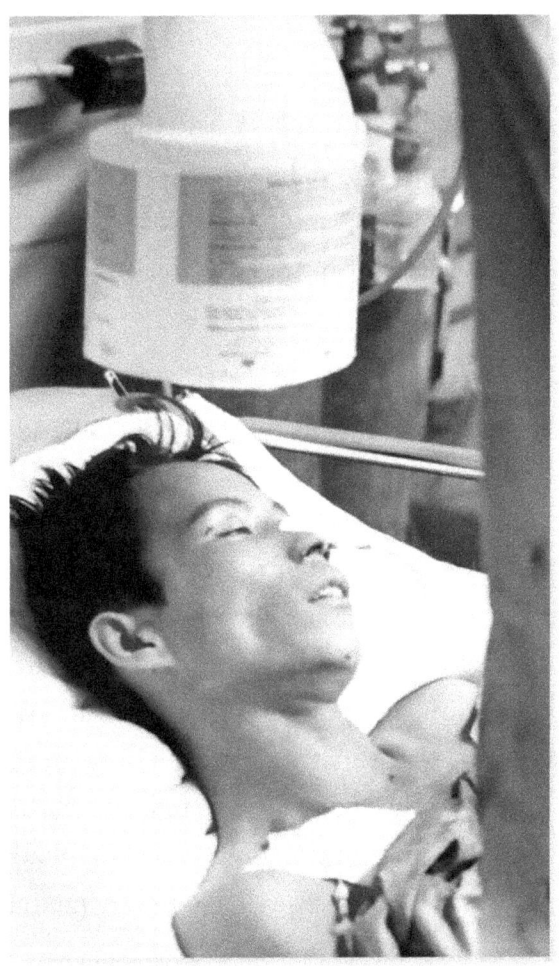

Huy near the end of his time with a CIDEX bottle
overhead helping him to breathe moist oxygen.

The next shift I worked, I noticed a Vietnamese woman, quite pregnant, looking in the window from the ward. It turned out to be Huy's' wife, eight months pregnant with their fifth child. My heart broke; Huy's chances of survival or rehab of any sort were practically nil. What would become of her and the children? I put him as close to the window as I could. I couldn't possibly let her in because the space was so tight. The Vietnamese common knowledge of sterile techniques was virtually nonexistent, and I was responsible for two other patients. The spiders were there, but I couldn't discard all our protocols; I had to try to keep things as clean as possible. Frustration and helplessness seemed to come with the job. Huy lived for ten more days and died of infection. His wife never left the window. We fed her and gave her a pallet on the floor, and lots of hugs and hand squeezes. I was not there for his passing; I have never forgotten his wife's haunting eyes.

Once at the beginning of a night shift, I got a call from Dr. Rocky. He was a rounded, jolly fellow, a general surgeon with wife and kiddos in the States. He had fallen in love with a 16-month-old baby girl. She was badly burned and he wanted my extra bed in the Burn Unit. I turned him right down; how could I possibly do that baby justice? She was awake and needed constant care and *no* spiders. We worked out a plan. Rocky would admit the baby in the ICU right outside my door and he would take care of her himself, as the ward was full, with only two nurses on duty. This baby needed someone with it every minute and it would be Dr. Rocky and the baby's mama. I peeked out my window constantly that night to see how they were doing. Mom on one side of the crib and Rocky's large form leaning over the other.

In the morning, heading to bed, I stopped there first. I knew Rocky had moved the baby from its bed to his lap several hours ago. I didn't know why. As I came out my door, I saw the tableau before me; huge Rocky sitting in a chair, baby on his lap, his hand on the mother's head, the mother on the floor at his feet, her head resting in his lap, one arm hugging his legs, the other caressing her dead baby. They were both crying, the mother wailing. I approached them, putting my arms around them, kissing them all on their foreheads. Without a word, I walked out into the heat, heading for bed. There were no words for that scene, only tears.

CHAPTER 6

THIS AND THAT

REST AND RECUPERATION

During my time in Vietnam, nurses were allowed three Rest and Recuperations (R&R's). I went alone for a week to Hong Kong and Chiang Mai, Thailand and got a much-needed reprieve. The most fun, though, was two weeks at a sheep ranch in Australia, a program put together by the Australian government. It was a lovely time with a young family and lots of baby lambs. My only complaint was the lamb's liver for breakfast.

In country, we needed breaks too, and this is where the helicopter pilots came in. They had an NCO (non-commissioned officers) club oddly enough right next to my hooch, so I saw these boys often. They were dear and always ready for a good time, having one of the most exciting and horrific jobs in Vietnam. Twelve thousand helicopters were deployed and almost half never came back. They brought in our patients under incredible circumstances. To this day, if I hear a helicopter, I have a flashback: it's a Huey helicopter like they had in Vietnam, and the sound will bring me to my knees.

Back in the days of naive, invincible youth, I was thrilled if a helicopter pilot would offer to take us to Vung Tau, where there was an Australian R&R center and we could swim in the hot South China Sea. It was such a change, with no one needing our medical attention and no one dying. We loved it! Later, some of the pilots

Huey helicopters affect people differently; to me it meant incoming wounded and sorrow, to others it was escape and hope for the future.

even rented a villa, complete with caretaker, and would leave us there alone for our almost two days off.

As a woman I was constantly being hit on. There were 15,000 women compared to 2.5 million GI's in Vietnam during the course of the war. I won't say I didn't have a few trysts and even fell in love a few times, but the amount of groping and sexual comments were a bit overwhelming and you needed to be on your guard all the time. Having a villa for a few days with no men was bliss!

LARRY THE LOBSTER

At some point during my first six months in country, I and two of my ward mates got the crazy idea of getting a standby flight on a fixed wing to Cam Ranh Bay were the American R&R center was located and the beaches were lovely. Well, all I remember of the place is that it was bloody hot. We tried to stay covered from the sun and going in the water was like taking a hot bath. We headed back to the airport burnt and exhausted. There were only three of us and the one working that night got the only empty seat on the next flight to Saigon. So that left Larry and me. Larry, I will tell you resembled a boiled lobster; his pain was incredible, and he was a bit woozy. I went right into nurse mode with cold cloths and a bit of aspirin.

We waited and waited for that next flight with two empty seats. We both worked the next morning shift, and some sleep would have been real nice. Finally, we did get on a plane, but too late, we arrived in Saigon after curfew. Yikes! What were we going to do!? We had to be at work at 7 a.m. It seemed impossible to spend the night at the Saigon airport and hitch a ride in the morning. We were burnt and covered with sand, a bad combination. I was dreaming of a cool shower. I stood in the airport with tears starting to flow, looking overwhelmed and frantic. I looked up and saw a General heading towards me. I panicked a bit because everything we had done that day was a bit illegal, including socializing with Larry a draftee, an enlisted man. Instead of being chastised, as I expected, he was quite nice and asked me what the problem was, and I spilled the beans, telling him all. He was lovely, and said, "No problem at all. I have a private helicopter and pilot right outside and he would get us back safely." What a gem. We were whisked away to the 24th Evac Hospital helipad and needed to dash instantly to the O_2 tank shed, so that the staff checking out the helicopter arrival didn't see us.

We made it to work in the morning, moving gingerly, especially Larry.

SHIT HAPPENS

This next incident wasn't exactly fun, but it was an adventure. The sewage system backed up at the hospital, flooding the wards. Suddenly, we had wards full of hepatitis patients, a disease spread by feces; this was *not* a good situation at all. The order came to evacuate the hospital; easier said, than done! Assessments, paperwork, transportation. Who would take them? A good number went to the hospital down the road, the 93rd Evac, but not too many, as they needed space for more incoming wounded. The alternative was moving the patients to other hospitals in Vietnam, Japan, and Germany. It was a nightmare. Luckily, I was not part of that administrative mess. I was as usual taking care of patients, but now slogging around in sewer water. We packed up and shipped out all the Stryker patients and most of the comatose ones, but some were just too fragile to move, so we waded around and took care of them. We were continuously washing our hands and trying not to breathe. Both doors to the Ward were open with the corpsmen trying to sweep all the shit outside.

My dear friend Teddy, a nurse known to speak her mind, spent a full shift literally shoveling shit off the ward and then went back to her hooch to shower and sleep, only to find her room and black shag carpet covered in sewage. She came back to the ward loudly voicing her complaints; she was exhausted and filthy, so I sent her to my hooch, which amazingly was *not* filled with sewage.

I believe the cause was found and the problem solved within 24 hours, but the aftermath and cleanup went on for weeks. Our cement floor turned into vinyl tiles, with the evidence at least hidden if not completely purged.

THE ATROCIOUS BOB HOPE SHOW

We were so excited! Half the staff was off duty for the Bob Hope show being held in Long Binh; some had the day off, others of us were just getting off the night shift and would shortchange ourselves on sleep. I rushed back to my hooch to get ready. We were going to wear civilian clothes, a rare treat.

To my horror my bedroom door was locked from the inside. How could that be? Now, we often let the corpsmen sleep in our beds while we worked because we had air conditioning and they sweltered, but that was usually for the hot, hot, day sleeping and they were usually on the ward by the time we left to go to bed. I couldn't remember making this arrangement with anyone, and they weren't answering my pounding on the door, so what was up? I raced around to my window outside and climbed up on the sandbags, going halfway up the wall, and peered in my tiny window. Lo and behold, there was an inert man in my bed whom I had never seen before. What the heck? I wanted to go to the show, starting in a few hours, and I needed to shower and change. I called the MP's for help. They arrived and extracted this man, still quite drunk who had wondered into the nurses quarters looking for action. I guess I had forgotten to lock the door and he passed out in my bed. I always locked that door as I slept, and never again forgot to lock up when I left for work.

Shortly, the crew met to wait for our ride to the show, all of us in our civvies, excited to be in something other than OD green fatigues with jungle boots. Our joy lasted about five minutes when the chief came by and ordered us back into our fatigues. We changed, but I still had on hair ribbons to remain festive.

Ward 5 crew headed out to the Bob Hope show. That's me in the center, with the hair ribbons.

Changing clothes made us a bit later for the show than we wanted to be. We were let off right behind the stage, so we had to join the audience from the front. It was a huge crowd; some had even climbed telephone poles for a better view. We were looking for our boys, our sweet patients, so that we could sit with them, with our corpsmen forever at our sides guarding us from the groping hands.

As soon as we rounded the corner of the stage, the entire audience stood up and cheered. We immediately turned to the stage because we thought the show had started, we were late! *Nothing* was on stage. They were cheering for *us*, their beloved nurses! What a moment. It made us cry. We nestled down amongst our patients in the broiling sun and waited and waited. The patients had the best seats (on the ground) but with the best view. Some of the fellows were looking a bit bedraggled because of the heat and the wait, so our crew started checking them and giving out water.

Finally, a large group of civilians came in and asked us to move back. They quickly erected a huge platform for the TV cameras. We could now see nothing. Prime seats were gone, we had no place to move, and it was mobbed. We listened and fumed through the show. It was a show for fame and fortune for the stars; the fighting men and wounded be damned. I still get upset thinking of it. I never watched another Bob Hope show and told everyone of this atrocity.

The Bob Hope show, Christmas Day 1970.

UNDERWEAR

Just a note on clothing: we lived in OD (olive drab) fatigues with wool socks, jungle boots and a boonie hat. The women had special fatigues with a panel in the blouse front, so there was no peeking through the snaps. We had long sleeves that were rolled up for work and put down for sun protection. The blouse had loops for scissors and any other accoutrements that one used often. The pants had side snaps. It was a practical outfit. I loved the boots; they were lightweight and comfortable and the socks quite cushy. That 12-hour shift was long with rarely a moment for sitting, and feet were important. We wore this outfit to work and anytime we left the base. The hat was used only for the sun and was loved by all. Some of the nurses wanted to retain a bit of style, so they wore their own socks. You could barely see them, so they weren't chastised, but it gave them a bit of a lift. I thought the army issue was more comfy, so I stuck with them. Underwear was not issued to women so you could get real fancy if you wanted, which I did for a while.

Alas, nice underwear was not practical. After each shift your entire outfit including boots was placed outside your hooch bedroom door. You were glad to do it, because they were covered with yuck from the ward and you couldn't get them off fast enough to jump into the shower. A lovely Vietnamese woman picked up your filthy clothes and put a washbasin in the shower and squatted down and scrubbed them, and washed and shined your boots. These were then placed on the rolls of barbed wire that surrounded your hooch to broil in the sun, and to get a few tiny holes from the barbs. Each evening your immaculate ironed uniform and shined boots were right outside your door.

The problem with the nice underwear was that it had disappeared. Now, did a GI take it, or did the washerwoman? It would sell nicely on the black market. Not wanting to make a fuss, I wrote to my mother to send me the biggest, most boring underpants she could find, and they never went missing again.

Clothes and bedding drying outside the nurses' hooches.

Getting the blood and yuck off the boots.

THE TANK

We wore civilian clothes only for private parties, or to go to a club or to the Chinese restaurant on base. This was the 1970's and miniskirts were in style, so one evening another nurse Patti and I decided to go eat at the officer's club. We dressed in the style of the day and stood outside the hospital to get a ride. Any nurse was always picked up by the first thing going by, even if in the wrong direction. Well, the first thing going by was a tank. The door to a tank is up on top and it's a long way up. There were at least four guys in the tank all eager to help us up and then down into the depths of the tank. Well, we tried to protect our modesty as best we could, I being thankful for my mother's gift of granny pants under my dress. The boys were real sweet and thrilled to help us. The officers at the club heard the tank approaching and came out to investigate, so we had twice the audience for the decent! No problem with invitations to dinner and drinks after that entrance! We wore fatigues for our next night out at the club.

Patti and I heading for the Officer's Club.

CHAPTER 7

WHERE WAS THE COMPASSION?

In compassion, when we feel with the other, we dethrone ourselves from the center of our world and we put another person there.

— KAREN ARMSTRONG

There were times when I found compassion to be missing and it still haunts me a bit. I know I was raised to be caring to everyone, and I realize that some have had hateful upbringings, so I should forgive them, for my own sake, and I have, but it's been a long time coming. I was angry way too long after leaving that war. I couldn't even say the word "Vietnam" for ten years, without an outburst or tears. I will tell you the stories and try to leave them behind.

CARELESS HOMICIDE

Once I came out of the medication room and saw a substitute corpsman cleaning up a patient. He was alone and hadn't activated the emergency bowel movement team. His patient was a very young, under 15-year-old ARVN (Army of the Republic of Vietnam) soldier. He was a tiny little guy, totally comatose, with a tracheotomy, but breathing well on his own. I noticed immediately that his tracheotomy was smashed into a pillow when he was turned for cleaning — he couldn't breathe. I ran to the bed, yelling at the corpsman, but I was too late, the boy was quite dead. The corpsman looked up at me and said, "Oh well, no loss, he was just a damn gook." I reported him immediately to the commanding officer of the hospital who just said, "We're lucky it wasn't a GI." I'm not sure that the corpsman was even reprimanded.

A POWERFUL PATRIARCH

One night an older Vietnamese gentleman was admitted to Ward 5, a quadriplegic with a brain stem injury, who would never be able to breathe without a respirator. In the times and under the circumstances, he would not live. The family was informed of the situation. As he was the patriarch of a large, very respected family, the family member accompanying him went to Saigon to spread the word. I also went to Saigon the next day on baby business, and on my return to the base, I spotted a big commotion at one of the front gates. I approached and saw this gentleman's daughter and perhaps 8 to 10 other family members. The Military Police didn't want to let them in. I told them the situation and said that I would be responsible for all the folks. I immediately found a ride for them, as the hospital was a several-mile walk and there were old and young alike in the group. I dropped the family off at Ward 5 and proceeded to my hooch to get ready for the night shift in four hours.

At 7 p.m. I passed about 8 or 9 of these people out in front of the ward. We had only ten patients on the ward at the time, so it seemed practically empty. A screen surrounded the patriarch with two family members tending him; he was not visible from the nurse's desk. At report, the charge nurse was complaining about all the damn gooks trying to invade her ward and she was tired of this old man who should already be dead. Why didn't they just take him off the respirator and why should the other patients have to watch this grieving drama?

I didn't say a word to her and just let her get out of there as fast as possible.

I moved the dying man out into the middle of the ward, folding the screen out of the way. All but two of our patients were comatose. The patriarch was very alert, and I checked with the other awake patient and he was cool with a bit of a wake.

I welcomed the rest of the family in, they were so grateful. I got hugs. Thank goodness they had brought food and water, as none had been offered in my absence. They did a beautiful little ceremony and all kissed Papa goodbye. There was a tiny bit of wailing, but didn't we all feel like doing that? They were gone in half an hour, their goodbyes said and Papa at peace. It was very unusual, but they left a small girl with her Grandpa to watch over him, as he said that he would die that night. I made a little bed for the child near her Grandpa and thought to myself it could be days if not weeks until he died. He was a healthy, robust man when he was shot. He was being ventilated with a mechanical respirator and was turned frequently to prevent pneumonia and bedsores. He was also getting fluids and food. I thought perhaps he could be moved eventually to the Vietnamese recovery ward.

Ah, Sara, you were young and dumb; that dear old man was dead by morning. I watched him fade all night, his skin tone turning darker every hour. He was willing himself to death, and I believe happy with his task. I watched him in wonder, never interfering, quite in awe. I brought his grandbaby over for a final kiss and his family picked up his body the next morning. Why was half an hour so much for that nurse to give to that family? He needed their goodbyes to find his way home. Compassion can be so simple.

STAND UP FOR THE HAUGHTY

I heard this story from a nurse friend; it happened right before I arrived in country. There was a little Vietnamese boy perhaps ten years old who oddly enough fell off a swing, resulting in a compound fracture of the tibia (lower leg). He was operated on, but for some reason the wound had a difficult time healing. He was on the orthopedic ward for months, so his family could not stay the whole time and he was adopted by the ward crew and dearly loved. One day the orthopedic surgeon decided that the wound would never heal, and the leg should be amputated. OK, that is usually a sound decision and a treatment to save a life. However, this child was not dying, and the doctor wanted to do it without informing the parents. He knew best: this was a war zone, and he was the surgeon, and he was in charge. The surgery was scheduled; the nurses could not talk him out of his rash decision. On the day of surgery, the entire staff of the orthopedic ward, night shift, day shift and people with the day off surrounded that child's bed and fed him as much as he would eat.

You are no doubt aware that you cannot have anesthesia on a full stomach, so the surgery was delayed. The parents were contacted and declined the surgery. Escalated ego is a terrible trait in a doctor.

CHILD SOLDIER

One child I remember particularly on Ward 3 was about 14 years old and a Viet Cong soldier. He had a frag wound to the groin right next to his genitalia. I could put my fist in the wound and see his hipbone. He was terrified and in agony. A screen was put around him "so as not to upset the GI's." I took it right down; he was a patient and a child and wasn't armed, and he was cuffed to the bed. He deserved to be cared for, and the other patients didn't need to be told he was a Viet Cong. I looked up one day to see a new corpsman starting to rinse his wound. The boy had not been medicated; it would be torture! I was so glad I had removed the screen and caught this action. I dismissed the corpsman with a few choice words, medicated the child, and returned an hour later and gently washed the wound myself. Not a sound came from his mouth, and I know it hurt like hell; he was terrified of a reprimand. He got only loving care from me; he was not my enemy, only another victim of this ghastly war. He was sadly, on recovery, being sent to a Vietnamese prison hospital; who knows what fate awaited him there? I guarded and cared for him for the rest of his stay with us. His eyes, watching my every move, were filled with appreciation and I have never forgotten them.

KIDNAPPED BABY

I found a home in Iowa for a beautiful 13-month-old baby girl, full Vietnamese. I don't remember what she came in for, but she had been in the Vietnamese convalescent ward for a long time. Her potential new papa visited often, and I was helping him with his paperwork. He was due to leave the country within the month and was thrilled to be taking back this precious treasure to his wife. Scads of people knew what was happening and were overjoyed for the two of them. Three weeks before the big event, the baby disappeared. I rushed to the chief's office, a woman, for an explanation. "Oh, the ward was pretty full, and she was healed, so we sent her to an orphanage up north." "You knew about the adoption?" I exclaimed, in shock. "Oh, yeah, but we already have too many immigrants in the US. We certainly don't need any more Vietnamese."

I got the name of the town and the orphanage to the father, and I sincerely hope he found her. I like to picture her standing in a cornfield, grinning.

I thought of this child and Kevin as the chief nurse told me at my exit interview that she was never so glad to see a nurse leave her charge. I agreed with her completely. I was quite a thorn in her compassionless side.

CHAPTER 8

PATTI'S STORY

The following three sections were written by my Vietnam nurse colleague and friend Patti Hill, now Patricia Hill-VanderMolen. They serve as companion pieces to my narrative.

A SLOW DAY AT THE WAR

It'd been a slow day at The War. We tended to talk of The War as though it was an event or a show and today the litter stands were empty in the preop ward. There was plenty of time to read the *Stars and Stripes* and find out how light the casualties had been for the week even though we'd treated more than that number at our hospital alone and we were just one of several. I'd been placed in an unwanted position of head nurse of preop/postop ward where we'd receive the guys right after the emergency room to await surgery and then take care of them when they'd been operated on. Not too much going on that day, it was one of those slow days.

There'd been a skirmish somewhere in an unknown location, accessible enough by helicopter to bring the wounded to the 24th Evac. We'd heard the call on the radio first and the emergency room alerted us that the war had "picked up." Sort of like the weather, a high-pressure area or something…but the slow day at The War was soon to be over.

It wasn't long before the first several litter stands were covered with litters of men in olive drab and dirt and blood — basic cases, simple frag wounds, some gunshot wounds, GSW for short, of the abdomen but relatively simple repairs on young otherwise healthy men. But they came and they came and there were more until there wasn't an empty litter stand available and only one nurse and two corpsmen for the entire task. And each one that came after was more severe, a spurting GSW of the head, chest wounds with tubes exiting every orifice, amputees who'd left their legs in the emergency ward… masses of them. The simple frag wounds were pushed further back to put the critical guys up front on the stands. And then *they* were brought in. Amongst all the injured GI's, three other casualties were picked up by the choppers — three Viet Cong soldiers who'd done some of the damage.

Initially they were in the middle line of people waiting for OR but as each new arrival was brought in, their litters were carried further to the back. Despite their serious wounds, we had stabilized them with fluids and blood and the immediate danger was past for the time being. But with every fresh GI that was brought in, I looked back on this trio and blamed them.

Until this point in my life, I'd never felt a real hate for another human being regardless of who they were. But this day was different…despite having been sent extra staff, I was running from litter to litter, pumping blood into pale bodies, trying to keep life going until the repairs could be made and each time I'd look back on my trio, angry that they'd put us all through this. At the height of the chaos, other nurses and corpsmen came in to lend a hand for a while. As I reached trembling for the narcotics drawer, I muttered to a friend that I was so afraid there weren't enough of us to save them all. And each time I looked towards my trio, blaming, blaming…

A helicopter Major strode onto the ward after he'd unloaded the last of the casualties out of the fire zone. Instantly, he spoke for all the Americans on the ward "We can't have this" and he and his men took the three Viet Cong to their helicopters to drop them off at the ARVN hospital. A relief came to us all, but later when The War slowed down again, I realized the significance of his move; the transport meant a sure death for these three men, the hated trio, as the ARVN hospital was not as benevolent as ours had been towards the enemy in less stressed times. And here I was, a nurse who'd found how one can hate someone you don't know just because he wasn't one of us. And yet we had inflicted the same damage to them. I'd thought of the other times I'd taken care of the enemy and had relayed to them the feeling of the hospital as a neutral zone, that as a nurse I took care of people and I didn't take sides; we had hurt each other and my job was to heal. But this time had been different: there were so many casualties and there were three to blame. I could only see the pain on our side and not the pain on theirs. Perhaps this is what makes a war viable, the ability to hate what is not yours or to see only one side and feel only one direction of pain.

For one day, The War had picked up and for a brief time I had felt hate. I didn't want to ever feel it again.

SECOND TOUR AND AFTER

I was 21 and barely a year out of nursing school when I went to Vietnam for my first tour at Qui Nhon in 1968. In all, I spent 27 months there, having extended that first tour for three months. I wanted to be a part of our nation's history, but early in that tour, my view of the war changed and I wanted this war to end. When I returned to the States, I was spat upon and called a whore. I marched in the peace protests. During that year stateside, I felt so lost, the world I'd left fifteen months before was so different. I had no patience with frivolous things. In the war I had been involved with daily life-and-death decisions. I returned to Long Binh, Vietnam one year later, remembering only the camaraderie and good times. At the end of my first week back, I sat on my bunk crying, "What have I done? I forgot that this was Hell." And with the next breath declared to myself that I'd better wipe those tears because I had 51 more weeks to go. I also promised myself that when I returned this time, that regardless how lost I felt, I would do all the things I dreamed of doing, that I wouldn't allow myself to be forever tied to this war. I wanted to ensure that Vietnam would not be the defining experience of my life.

I kept that promise. I skydived, backpacked a thousand miles of the Appalachian Trail, whitewater canoed the wonderful rivers of Tennessee, Georgia, and North Carolina, awakened from my sleeping bag with my dog to beautiful splendor, lived in a VW van during a 3-month "retirement" trip with my best friend and her dog which took us throughout the Southwest and up to Alaska, cross country skied and solo winter camped in Yellowstone, worked seasonally as a Park Ranger during mini-retirements from nursing, wintered in Maine, and summered in New Orleans (the rich do it the other way!).

It wasn't until I turned 40, living in New Orleans, that the war years resurfaced so strongly that I could no longer fight back the nightmares. Perhaps it was the oppressive heat of Louisiana which reminded me of Vietnam or perhaps it was just that I slowed down long enough to stop running from my memories. On my 40th birthday, awakening in tears, I pulled the book, *Long Time Passing: Vietnam and the Haunted Generation* (Myra MacPherson) from my bookshelf. After the first several pages, I realized what the tears meant: I was crying for all those who would never turn 40, whose memory I could not erase, and that it was time to open an old scar and debride that wound that I'd carried for nearly two decades. I went to a Vietnam Veteran's group and for some time felt at peace until the Gulf War reactivated the nightmares and smells of that earlier time.

After much support from my boyfriend (and now, husband) and therapy, I'm finally at peace.

The day of the women's statue dedication in Washington, DC was especially healing. So many people of all walks of life who came to say "Thank You" meant so much to me: the Indian honor guard who escorted the statue, the Arsenio salutes "whoop, whoop, whoop," the widow who came to thank us, the man in a wheelchair saluting us as we marched, the numerous ex- and current GIs…I thank all of you, for you have sealed my peace.

Many times, I've encountered comments that make me realize that most people don't understand what experiences we nurses had in Vietnam. One friend tried to tell me that his year in Germany was much "worse" than my two years in Vietnam because he could have been called up anytime! Another comment was that I probably didn't see much as I was in a rear hospital. I began to put a lot of my residual memories into a prose poem called "Upon This Wall" which gives some indication of what the years in SICU, Preop, Postop and ER were like.

We returned to Vietnam in January 2000, not to relive old war memories but for our son, a four-month-old boy from Hanoi. It is very peaceful there now, and also, here.

UPON THIS WALL

MAY 1968 – SEPTEMBER 1969, QUI NHON

Upon this Wall is Lynn, 1 of 6, whose APC hit a land mine, burning and maiming those inside, who after days of massive infusions of IV fluids, antibiotics, pain meds, and dressing changes over scalded flesh, died in Japan 2 days after leaving us.

Upon this Wall are 2 of 4, 4 with high thoracic spinal cord injuries, 4 in a row on SICU, 2 Americans, 2 Vietnamese, dying slowly one by one, comforted only by a touch on the shoulder or hair; 1, the last, who died so frightened.

Upon this Wall is a sergeant in his 40s, a father, killed not by enemy fire but by a helicopter tail rotor.

Upon this Wall is a young lieutenant with minor frag wounds whose soul drowned in a rain puddle in which he fell.

Upon this Wall is Bob, who survived his wounds but died of a pulmonary embolus as he talked with Deanna.

Upon this Wall is one from the bunker: a crew-top, sandy-haired young man who ran from its safety to retrieve his M-16 during a Viet Cong attack on our compound, who survived numerous lung surgeries but died of a ruptured spleen, misdiagnosed as his "heart giving out."

Upon this Wall is one alone, a young soldier in isolation, who died of Typhoid fever after numerous blood transfusions and surgeries to resect the bleeding Peyer's patches in his bowel. Each time we thought we could save him, but we were wrong.

Upon this Wall is David, run over by a deuce-and-a-half while he slept in its shade, who bartered a kiss for pain medicine, but whose crush injury was too great.

Upon this Wall is Stanley, so terrified of dying, whose hand we held, who did not die alone.

Within this memory is a 7-year-old girl, "Pigtails," whose left arm & leg were ripped open by the deuce-and-a-half that dragged her through the streets of Qui Nhon, who comforted me with her smile as much as I comforted her with my hugs, whose death seemed so unfair.

Within this memory is the young woman in the light blue aldi which covered her napalm scarred body, who we helped to walk again.

Within this memory is a Viet Cong man, thrown on a stretcher from a helicopter hovering over our landing zone.

Within this memory are soldiers whose "blindness" we cured by leaving things out of reach, who once found out, were returned to battle.

Within this memory are 13-hour days and 6-day weeks, assisted with Ritalin to wake up and Seconal to sleep until exhaustion dictated only sleep and work, no time to dream, no time to heal, no time to cry.

Within this memory are young men, quadriplegic and paraplegic, on Stryker frames with Crutchfield tongs.

Within this memory are battles against systemic bacterial infections fought with "10 of Pen and 2 of Chloro;" the smells of burned, charred flesh: weeping fasciotomies that relieved the pressure on the bloated limbs; the smell of pseudomonas from tracheas; a surgeon arriving in country with a suitcase of Sulfamylon cream, the latest defense.

SEPTEMBER 1970 – SEPT 1971, LONG BINH

Upon this Wall are 5 of 6, 5 who died because the helicopter pilot wanted a photo of them going under a bridge.

Upon this Wall are 1 and others, 1 who survived the plane crash but had 100% 3rd degree burns, who could not see because of the swelling, who did not know, who was comforted by morphine and a soft voice. One who finally died after the fluids were shut off and the morphine increased. One who never had the chance to say "good-bye."

Upon this Wall are many "expectants," men with severe head injuries whose lives had ended before their bodies, who were put behind screens as we cared for those who might survive.

Upon this Wall is a soldier with an arm infected from dirty heroin needles, who died on the operating table with a heart full of pus.

Upon this Wall is a warrant officer helicopter pilot killed from a rocket that went off when he walked in front of a Cobra.

Upon this Wall are a group of men, bunched together at the end of the ER, gray baby faces, already dead, no time to mourn, time only for the living.

Within this memory is a young man pleading with me "My leg, my leg, don't take my leg" as I snipped the remaining tissue with my bandage scissors; No time for comfort, only time to stop the bleeding and then send him past the dead into surgery.

Within this memory is a Viet Cong who eluded Cobra rockets, who might have escaped, who the fatherless pilot saluted.

Within this memory is a young black soldier who cried "How can we be over here fighting for their freedom when my people aren't free!" whom I didn't have an answer for.

Within this memory are 3 Viet Cong on stretchers who kept being pushed towards the back of my ward as more and more casualties came in until there was barely room to walk; the shame later that evening of feeling hatred towards other human beings for all the carnage they had caused when we had done the same to their side.

Within this memory is a 16-year-old Viet Cong whose hand I held, whose fears I calmed because I could no longer hate.

Within this memory is a young ARVN soldier whose lower body was amputated from above the hip bone, who received so much blood that he no longer had any clotting ability, who slowly bled out of every orifice, until we finally said "no more."

Within this memory is a magazine reporter, whose death set off a feud amongst ARVN troops about his remaining possessions.

Within this memory is a soldier, paralyzed and missing an arm, who made it home, who drove a van and went parasailing with another nurse after the War, who one day couldn't take the pain anymore and blew himself away.

FINISHING SCHOOL: COMBAT VETERAN'S GROUP, NEW ORLEANS 1987

Upon this Wall are 3 of 6, men whose helicopter crashed, 3 who were rescued by a sergeant who blamed himself for only rescuing half before it burst into flames, who taught me how we blame ourselves for those we lost but can't see those we saved.

Upon this Wall is all but 1, 1 man evac'd out due to wounds the day before his entire group was extinguished, who carries the burdens of so many friends' memories, who taught me of the guilt of surviving.

EPILOGUE: PEACE

Missing from this Wall are the others, the 5 of 6, the 1 of all, those who survived.

Within this memory is a WW II soldier who remembered wanting rest after a long battle in France, who finally found rest after his long battle with cancer on a VA ward, who had a nurse who could listen and guide because of a burned soldier in Vietnam.

Upon this Wall are stories of how we learned about respirators and ventilators and burn treatment and TPN and helicopter evacuations, and numerous medical advances that we use in hospitals today. And yet, Upon this Wall is the pain of nurses who judge themselves with every new bit of knowledge we learn, who think we should have known what Kubler-Ross and medical science would later teach us, who would come to know that we were human in an inhumane place.

NOVEMBER 11, 1993, DEDICATION OF WOMEN'S STATUE, WASHINGTON, DC.

They said, "Thank You."

EPILOGUE

There was never a good war or a bad peace.
— BENJAMIN FRANKLIN

I spent a year and five days in Vietnam. I stayed the extra five days because a nursing school buddy was arriving in country, and I wanted to be sure that she got my refrigerator and electric frying pan and a few other hard-to-find commodities. And I wanted to hug her and wish her well.

You'd think that after such a horrendous year, I would be thrilled to be leaving Vietnam behind. I had thought that, too; we even kept calendars marking our days remaining, but it was not the case.

We were given a month of leave before reporting to our next assignment stateside. I planned on a bit of holiday in Japan and spent much of it sadly waiting at the airport for a plane to Alaska to see my sister. I was not in a holiday mood, and I thought that I would get understanding at my sister's: not so, nor at my parents'. In truth, no one could understand what I had just lived through — no one except someone who had lived it, such as another nurse, a doctor, or a corpsman. So, I spent my month with a nursing school buddy who went to Vietnam six months before me. I sat on her deck and stared into space. We didn't need to talk, we knew.

It may seem strange, but I wanted to go back. I wanted to work with that Angel I met at the orphanage in Saigon. I wanted to finish my job, the job that I always felt I never finished during that whole year in Vietnam and for years afterward. I felt I needed to do more; that's why nurses and corpsmen re-upped. I remembered my friend Patti's hard re-up and knew it would be a mistake, but I felt useless stateside.

I felt scorned upon my return to the States, even spit at. This was not a popular war. I never said the word "Vietnam" for ten years without crying or being chastised. I went on to midwifery school and countless jobs, always feeling like an outsider. My stateside patients got so much less compassion from me; they weren't living in cardboard boxes. They had food to eat, and no one was trying to kill them. Why were they complaining? I was a terrible employee. I finally escaped to Alaska where I could work alone, and the healing could begin. Thank you to many of my kind friends and family who never knew the agony I suffered but supported me nonetheless because they could see the real me underneath.

In Alaska I became a homeopath with 2,000 patients, and I loved the work. I loved helping people. I could effect real change. I taught my classes in homeopathy, empowering people to help themselves and their families. I could work alone with patients coming to my house, so I could be with my children or my own thoughts between patients. My two children and my second husband, together with my delightful small Alaska town, have sustained me and given me great joy.

Several years ago, my beautiful daughter was plucked from this earth by great evil, which triggered my dormant Agent Orange cancer. I have now entered hospice care, and I feel good that I have finally told my Vietnam truth. Thank you for reading it.

Homer, Alaska
December 2023

Sara passed on January 24, 2024, at home, after a long illness with bone cancer. Her family and friends celebrated her life with a funeral pyre on a sunny winter day in Kachemak Bay.

APPENDIX

MEDICAL AND OTHER ACRONYMS AND TERMS

Aldi (Áo dài) — A Vietnamese national garment consisting of a long split tunic worn over silk trousers. It can serve as formalwear for both men and women (Wikipedia)

APC — Armored Personnel Carrier

ARVN — Army of the Republic of (South) Vietnam

Deuce and a half — A two-and-a-half ton army truck

ER — Emergency Room

Foley catheter — A tube inserted through the penis into the urinary bladder, so as to continuously drain the bladder of urine

Frag wounds — Soft-tissue wounds caused by fragments of exploded ordinance

GI's — Slang term referring to U.S. military members

GSW — Gunshot wounds

Hooch — A slang term for the nurses' quarters at the 24th Evacuation Hospital

ICU — Intensive Care Unit

IM — Intramuscular, a shot injected into a muscle

IV — Intravenous line

OD — Olive drab, the color of the fatigue uniforms worn by most U.S. army soldiers in Vietnam

OR — Operating room

Peyer's patches — Thickenings of the intestinal wall

PRN — As needed, from the Latin phrase *pro re nata*

R&R — Rest and Recuperation. Slang term for free time often at a distant location, giving military personnel respite from the war

SICU — Surgical Intensive Care Unit

Stryker — A narrow two-layered stretcher that allows the patient to be completely turned over (see pages 7–8)

TB — Tuberculosis

TPN — Total parenteral nutrition (intravenous feeding), as with comatose patients

Tracheotomy — A surgical procedure where a hole (tracheostomy) is cut into the front of the trachea (windpipe) that allows the patient to breathe

Trach tube — A slang term for a tracheostomy tube, which is a tube placed in the tracheostomy opening in the trachea

ABOUT THE AUTHOR

Sara Berg was born in Wareham, Massachusetts on August 2, 1948, and grew up around the U.S. and in Germany as part of a large military family. The Army recruited her while she was in nursing school in Maryland. Sara had no idea how her life would change as a result. Sara, then 22, was posted for a year in Vietnam, 1970–71, where she tended to injured and dying soldiers, in many cases sharing the final words or being the final face a soldier saw before death.

Upon discharge, Sara completed midwifery training in Kentucky in 1976, but she found she couldn't focus and felt isolated and unsettled from her time in Vietnam. When her sister Mary, the first VISTA volunteer in Alaska, needed help as a new single mother, Sara joined her in the largest state. It was here in Alaska that Sara found herself.

Sara married and had two children, Gregory and Anesha ("Duffy"). Being a mother was Sara's true calling. She was a fun and adventurous parent, taking her children on outdoor trips around Alaska as well as on world travels — including to Thailand, Mexico, and Greece — so they could see the wider world beyond their own, and understand the common humanity that unites us all.

Six years after the divorce from her first husband, Sara met the love of her life, Ed Berg, in a homeopathy class he was teaching in Homer. Seeing how Ed could cure Duffy's chronic ear infections using homeopathy, Sara sought additional training. She wanted to stay at home with her children, so Sara started a homeopathic practice out of her home, which she ran for thirty years, lovingly ministering to local families and people who traveled hundreds of miles to see her. Duffy inherited Sara's compassionate nature, and the two spent many months caring for children at Nuestros Pequeños Hermanos, a large orphanage in Honduras.

Sara never knew she could write a book. But in the midst of the summer of 2023, during a period when she could do little else than endure a series of intense medical treatments, she wrote *Kissing Kevin* in three months, the words bursting out of her between doctors' appointments. She enjoyed every minute of it.

ABOUT CIRQUE PRESS

Cirque Press grew out of *Cirque*, a literary journal that publishes the works of writers and artists from the North Pacific Rim, a region that reaches north from Oregon to the Yukon Territory, south through Alaska to Hawaii, and west to the Russian Far East.

Cirque Press is a partnership of Sandra Kleven, publisher, and Michael Burwell, editor. Ten years ago, we recognized that works of talented writers in the region were going unpublished, and the Press was launched to bring those works to fruition. We publish fiction, nonfiction, and poetry, and we seek to produce art that provides a deeper understanding about the region and its cultures. The writing of our authors is significant, personal, and strong.

Sandra Kleven — Michael Burwell, publishers and editors
www.cirquejournal.com

BOOKS FROM CIRQUE PRESS

Apportioning the Light by Karen Tschannen (2018)

The Lure of Impermanence by Carey Taylor (2018)

Echolocation by Kristin Berger (2018)

Like Painted Kites & Collected Works by Clifton Bates (2019)

Athabaskan Fractal: Poems of the Far North by Karla Linn Merrifield (2019)

Holy Ghost Town by Tim Sherry (2019)

Drunk on Love: Twelve Stories to Savor Responsibly by Kerry Dean Feldman (2019)

Wide Open Eyes: Surfacing from Vietnam by Paul Kirk Haeder (2020)

Silty Water People by Vivian Faith Prescott (2020)

Life Revised by Leah Stenson (2020)

Oasis Earth: Planet in Peril by Rick Steiner (2020)

The Way to Gaamaak Cove by Doug Pope (2020)

Loggers Don't Make Love by Dave Rowan (2020)

The Dream That Is Childhood by Sandra Wassilie (2020)

Seward Soundboard by Sean Ulman (2020)

The Fox Boy by Gretchen Brinck (2021)

Lily Is Leaving: Poems by Leslie Ann Fried (2021)

One Headlight by Matt Caprioli (2021)

November Reconsidered by Marc Janssen (2021)

Callie Comes of Age by Dale Champlin (2021)

Someday I'll Miss This Place Too by Dan Branch (2021)

Out There In The Out There by Jerry McDonnell (2021)

Fish the Dead Water Hard by Eric Heyne (2021)

Salt & Roses by Buffy McKay (2022)

Growing Older In This Place: A Life in Alaska's Rainforest by Margo Wasserman Waring (2022)

Kettle Dance: A Big Sky Murder by Kerry Dean Feldman (2022)

Nothing Got Broke by Larry F. Slonaker (2022)

On the Beach: Poems 2016-2021 by Alan Weltzien (2022)

Sky Changes on the Kuskokwim by Clifton Bates (2022)

Transplanted by Birgit Lennertz Sarrimanolis (2022)

Between Promise and Sadness by Joanne Townsend (2022)

Yosemite Dawning by Shauna Potocky (2022)

The Woman Within by Tami Phelps and Kerry Dean Feldman (2023)

In the Winter of the Orange Snow by Diane S. Carpenter (2023)

Mail Order Nurse by Sue Lium (2023)

All in Due Time by Kate Troll (2023)

Infinite Meditations For Inspiration and Daily Practice by Scott Hanson (2023)

Getting Home from Here by Anne Ward-Masterson (2023)

Crossing the Burnside Bridge & Other Poems by Janice D. Rubin (2023)

A Variable Sense of Things by Ron McFarland (2023)

Tiny's Stories: An Athabascan Family on the Yukon River by Theresa "Tiny" Demientieff Devlin with Sam Demientieff (2024)

If Singing Went On by Gerald Cable (2024)

May the Owl Call Again: A Return to Poet John Meade Haines, 1924–2011 by Rachel Epstein (2024)

Out of the Dark: A Memoir by Marian Elliott (2024)

CIRCLES
ILLUSTRATED BOOKS FROM CIRQUE PRESS

Baby Abe: A Lullaby for Lincoln by Ann Chandonnet (2021)

Miss Tami, Is Today Tomorrow? by Tami Phelps (2021)

Miss Bebe Goes to America by Lynda Humphrey (2022)

MORE PRAISE FOR *KISSING KEVIN*

This is a story of war's dreadful toll on civilians and soldiers, and one person's attempts to mitigate its devastations. It was my privilege to watch as Sara responded to suffering with compassion, hard work, humor, rule-breaking, and fierce determination to be a force for good. Now, more than 50 years later, she vividly and eloquently describes life and work in an Army trauma center in Vietnam during the war.

> — Eleanor Frank Bond, PhD, RN, Professor Emeritus, University of WA School of Nursing; Former Captain, U.S. Army Nurse Corps, stationed at the 24th Evacuation Hospital, Long Binh, Vietnam

I worked side by side with Sara in Vietnam and she tells a story that the world needs to hear. Her book is accurate, concise, and heartbreaking. She shares with us the devastating toll of war to combat soldiers and their fellow sister and brother soldiers that care for them, along with the innocent local civilians caught in the fires of hell.

> — Theodora F. "Teddi" McLeskey, LTC(R), Army Nurse Corps

The moment I started reading and viewing the pictures, I was drawn back to the 24th Evac Hospital 1971 at Long Binh, Vietnam. The feeling it stirred was not particularly good, but I could not stop reading. This book is the real Vietnam.

> — Helen Schultz Buchner, Army Nurse Corps, classmate at Mercy Hospital in Baltimore and close friend since high school. Served in 1971–1972 at the 24th Evac Hospital, Long Binh, Vietnam

This book shows a bright light in the middle of war. The love and compassion of Sara and her fellow nurses is beyond belief. No matter what, they did everything they could to bring comfort to soldiers and children alike. This is a rare look into the other side of war. Sara brings us into the wards of injured soldiers and wounded children. This book will make you love the nurses for the angels they are. I laughed, I cried and couldn't put it down.

> — From my sister Trina Phipps

As a combat veteran I think I can speak for all of us "grunts" who experienced the horror and chaos of war when I say that when we got the wounded into a Medivac chopper, sometimes getting injured ourselves, we hoped and prayed they would make it to the dedicated medical personal at the Evac Hospitals. It was reassuring to know that we too could get the care of you wonderful people if we were injured. Whether friend or foe, young or old, an injured person deserves the best care possible.

We would experience the pain, suffering, and heartbreak for a relatively short period whereas you good people had to deal with it for a much longer time. I don't think any of us that went to Vietnam ever really left there after returning home. We carry the memories in us forever and can't ever forget. I'm so sorry that Agent Orange, Blue, PTSD, etc. has caused you, me, and all the rest of us so much sickness and pain. Your story has brought tears to my eyes and pain in my heart. You're such a compassionate, caring, and strong lady. Thank you so much from all of us.

— Philip Lee Sherwood, Sp. 4 C Co. 1–20 11th LIB Americal (23 Infantry) Division Vietnam, July 20, 1969–Sept. 16, 1970

Sara's love and care for the dying soldiers in Vietnam, children really, make it possible for the reader to enter the reality of war without shutting ourselves down. She brings us past the cold and distancing numbers we hear in the news to the real people — those injured and those brave enough to care for them. Surely it is the distancing of numbers that makes us tolerate the intolerable reality of war. Might Sara's compassionate touching of injured people make us sane again, and bring truth into actions for peace?

— Jean Burgess, friend

www.ingramcontent.com/pod-product-compliance
Lightning Source LLC
LaVergne TN
LVHW010334070526
838199LV00065B/5741